MW00785390

"A credible and provocative defense of the resurrection of Jesus Christ that deserves to be taken seriously by the academic community. The author brilliantly shows how the pagan myths of dying and rising gods lend support to the New Testament claim that Jesus rose bodily from the dead."

— *Donald G. Bloesch*
Emeritus Professor of Theology
University of Dubuque, Theological Seminary

"The central event on which Christianity stands or falls is the resurrection of Jesus from the dead. An event of such magnitude reveals as much about us who seek to understand it as it does about Jesus. ...McKenzie comes down solidly on the side of the bodily resurrection of Jesus, not as a variant of pagan resurrection myths, but as a fulfillment of them. This is a first-rate study of the resurrection, from start to finish."

— *James R. Edwards, Ph. D.*
Professor of Religion
Jamestown College

"Leon McKenzie has put his finger on something so evident to us now, but hidden a scant twenty years earlier: the massive presumptions which a purportedly "scientific" approach entails to matters humane and religious. He targets the presumptions operative in much recent and not-so-recent scripture scholarship regarding Jesus' resurrection, showing how their 'conclusions' followed not from the arguments put forward but from the presumptions assumed."

— *David Burrell, C. S. C.*
Hesburgh Professor of Philosophy and Theology
Notre Dame University

"Professor McKenzie furnishes his audience with an excellent antidote to the rationalist-naturalist premises of so much biblical criticism.

— *Francis Canavan, S. J.*
Professor Emeritus of Political Science
Fordham University

Pagan Resurrection Myths and the Resurrection of Jesus

A Christian Perspective

Leon McKenzie

BOOKWRIGHTS PRESS
of CHARLOTTESVILLE

Pagan Resurrection Myths and the Resurrection of Jesus: A Christian Perspective
Copyright © 1997, 2012 Bookwrights
All rights reserved under the International and Pan-American Copyright Conventions.

No part of this book may be reproduced in any form, or by any means, without prior
written permission from the publisher.

Southern Academic Editions

published by
Bookwrights Press
email: design@bookwrights.com

Printed in the United States of America
1 2 3 4 5 6 7 8

1-880404-13-3 (hardcover) O.O.P.
1-880404-24-9 (paper)
978-1-880404-23-2 (ebook)

Library of Congress Cataloging-in-Publication Data

McKenzie, Leon,
    Pagan resurrection myths and the Resurrection of Jesus : a Christian perspective /
Leon McKenzie.
        p.   cm. — (Southern academic editions)
    Includes bibliographical references and index.
        ISBN 1-880404- 24-9(alk. paper)
        1. Jesus Christ—Resurrection. 2. Resurrection--Comparative studies.   I. Title.
II. Series.
BT481.M293   1997   97-7135
232' .5—dc21   CIP

CONTENTS

"For that which happened on the 'third day' in Jerusalem is in the last analysis an experience of God which enters into the realm of things which cannot be proved, just as God himself is unprovable; it can be grasped only by faith."

—Pinchas Lapide, *The Resurrection of Jesus: A Jewish Perspective*

INTRODUCTION

The argument is sometimes made today that Jesus' bodily resurrection is "nothing but" another myth in a long line of myths. Even the pagans, it is observed, believed in resurrection myths. Notwithstanding this tendency (documented in Chapter One), the resurrection of Jesus is not viewed here in the interpretive framework of pagan myths; pagan myths of renewal are viewed in terms of the resurrection of Jesus. The Word of God was uttered decisively in history in the resurrection of Jesus thereby validating the whispered hints spoken in the myths of natural religion. Pagan myths of rebirth, sometimes called resurrection myths, played an important role in the economy of salvation history.

Pagan resurrection myths, in these pages, are interpreted as projections of a universal archetype of the human collective unconscious. In a sense, these myths may be understood to be authentically human to the point of reflecting all of the vagaries and ambiguities associated with being human. There is an element of truth in all resurrection myths; the truth, though, is masked in obscurity. The resurrection of Jesus, in turn, is viewed as the authentication of what Carl Jung called the resurrection archetype. I understand an archetype as a meaning structure of the human collective unconscious. The God who raised Jesus from the dead is the same God who created a world in which resurrection motifs abound and register in human experience. This is the same God who created the psychological mechanisms by which experiences of the resurrection motif are interpreted and transformed into myths. It is not surprising at all that some pagan resurrection myths broadly insinuate something about the resurrection of Jesus.

This introduction provides an overview of the themes of the book. An introductory presentation of a book's thematic design often makes the thesis of the book more intelligible from the outset and assists readers in getting to the core purpose of the work. The purposes of this book are several, but they all revolve around the central mystery of Christian faith, the resurrection of Jesus.

The first chapter of the book—"Questioning the Reality of Jesus' Resurrection"—begins with the fact that even some who call themselves Christian reject, as an actual event, the resurrection of Jesus. This situation is documented by means of brief critical reviews of A. N. Wilson's *Jesus: A Life,* Barbara Thiering's *Jesus and the Riddle of the Dead Sea Scrolls,* and Episcopal bishop John Spong's *Resurrection: Myth or Fact?* The claims of these books are shown to be grievously flawed.

Further, the books of these three authors, and the works of others who deny Jesus' bodily resurrection, are critiqued from the standpoint of the type of Biblical-historical research model employed. The rationalist-naturalist model used today by many scholars assumes *a priori* that all unusual events reported in the gospels must be explained without recourse to any transcendent cause. E.g., miracles do not happen and no one can rise from the dead. The resurrection of Jesus is rejected by somber scholars not as a conclusion based on the findings of their research, but instead as pseudo-conclusion founded on the often hidden assumptions of their research models. This is transparent to anyone familiar with research design theory and practice.

The distinction between the Christ of faith and the Jesus of history is also open to criticism. The assumptions upon which the portraits of the Jesus of history have been drawn are often vague. It seems, however, that what is written in the canonical gospels is routinely rejected as applicable to the Jesus of history. This results in depictions of the Jesus of history that are mostly self-portraits of the writers and variations on current ideological fads. As Albert Schweitzer commented nearly a century ago, those who write of the Jesus of history reveal more of themselves than the real Jesus. They also reveal their ideological predilections.

The nature of Biblical research is examined broadly in the first chapter. There is a research continuum ranging from the "hard" data of the systematic empirical sciences such as physics to the "soft" data of the so-called "social sciences." Some research findings support *conclusive* inferences; other research findings support *indicative* inferences. Still other findings are so mixed with surmises that inferences can be drawn only with many reservations. Biblical-historical research, for all of its importance, often yields conclusions that are simply *speculative*. Biblical research is weak in its conclusions. This is due to the fact that it is the kind of research wherein multiple weak theories abound. This is not to say that weak theories are bad. It is simply to note that some kinds of systematic research, *on the basis of the nature of the research itself*, are not as probative as others. Many of the books written in recent years that repudiate the traditional teaching about the resurrection of Jesus are speculative at best. Conclusions are often gratuitously given on the basis of the thinnest of conjectures. Historical-critical research accomodates presuppositions well.

The chapter concludes with an incident that occurred many years ago. A chance meeting of an older man on a train—someone who argued that Jesus was but another mythic figure like the pagan gods—awakened my interest in the question of the resurrection of Jesus. It was proved in a book titled *The Golden Bough*, the stranger claimed, that Jesus was but another mythic figure. My subsequent reading of *The Golden Bough* failed to confirm the older gentleman's verdict that Jesus is "nothing but" a mythic figure. While there are fragile but important continuities between pagan resurrection myths and the resurrection of Jesus (continuities that can be explained from a Christian perspective), the discontinuities are immense.

The second chapter is titled "Dying and Reviving Gods." One of the books that insinuated very strongly that the resurrection of Jesus was but another myth in a long line of myths was, as noted previously, was Sir James Frazer's *The Golden Bough*. This work, originally printed in eleven volumes toward the end of the last century, has enjoyed a long publishing history in one-volume editions. What Frazer intimated in the book regarding the resurrection of Jesus, in my view, has never been critiqued as thoroughly as one would wish, particularly the stories of dying and resurrected gods as prototypes of the resurrection of Jesus.

The dying and resurrected gods of Frazer's *The Golden Bough* bear little resemblance to the Jesus of the gospels and Christian tradition. The resurrection of Frazer's gods were not at all comparable to the resurrection of Jesus. The resurrections of Tammuz, Adonis, Astarte, Attis, Marsyas, Hyacinth, Osiris, Dionysus, and Demeter and Persephone are described. The resurrections or revivals of these gods possess as their primary character the quality of the ahistorical. These so-called resurrection events "occurred" not in historic time but only "once upon a time" in mythic images projected from the collective unconscious. The *differences* between the resurrections of the gods and the resurrection of Jesus are explicated in the second chapter. Early Christian worship, which reflects Christian belief, is compared and contrasted with pagan mystery religions. Contrary to popular assumptions, mystery religions were not religions in any univocal sense that allows comparison with the Jewish or Christian religions.

The idea of the universal archetype or universal psychic paradigm is treated in "The Resurrection Archtype," the third chapter. While there are major differences between Jesus' resurrection and the rebirths of pagan gods, there are also thematic *similarities*. Myths are viewed from my perspective as analogies or allegories that point to transcendental and universal truths. These myths are projections of universal archetypes. The ideas of C. G. Jung regarding the collective unconscious are examined briefly.

Jung believed the archetypes of the collective unconscious were innate. In my view, the capacity for the formation of the archetypes is innate but the archetypes themselves are constructed on the basis of universal human experiences. There are at least seven main resurrection motifs that occur continually and impactfully in human experience: 1) cycles of vegetation, 2) climactic/solar cycles, 3) daily cycles, especially the "dying" and "rising" of the sun, 4) stellar cycles, the disappearance and re-appearance of constellations, 5) the "death" of sleep and "rising" from sleep, 6) the waning and waxing of tribal/community fortunes, and 7) human mood cycles that can reflect moods ranging from depression to elation. Many additional death-resurrection motifs evidence the fact that death and resurrection constitute a primordial and fundamental theme manifested in the created world. The resurrection of Jesus, far from being "just another myth" is the validation of the essential meaning structures of the collective unconscious. Or, to put this another way, the most profound psychic meaning structures constituted within universal human experience exemplify the subjective correlative vis-a-vis Jesus' resurrection as something resembling an objective correlative. There is an excellent "fit" between the meaning structures formed in universal human experience and the resurrection of Jesus. This is not at all surprising to Christians who believe that the resurrected Jesus is God's decisive word in the dialogue between the God who created the cosmos, humankind, and psychic meaning structures or archetypes that derive from universal human experience.

The fourth chapter—"Resurrection Faith and Imagination"—suggests that many "modern" people are unable to believe in the bodily resurrection of Jesus not because of a lack of intellectual acumen nor because of moral flaws. Instead, they lack an adequate interpretive imagination. That is, their imaginations have been formed according to the suppositions of the modern secular era, a period of intellectual history also known as the Enlightenment. There is a genealogy of the distinctively modern secular imagination and this genealogy can be traced fairly well. The ideologies of a narrow rationalism, scientism, philosophical naturalism, materialism, atheism (together with atheism's cousins, agnosticism and Deism), and nihilism have fashioned the paradigmatic womb in which the modern secular imagination took form. It is not as if there have been large-scale intellectual conversions to these ideologies as such. On the contrary, the ideologies that have given rise to the modern secular imagination have been *enacted* unthinkingly as if they are true by millions of people in the contemporary world. The modern secular imagination has been formed on the basis of the actions of people and not necessarily on the grounds of their philosophical beliefs. Quite frequently their articulated beliefs have no relationship to their consistent patterns of behavior.

We have, fortunately, arrived at a point in intellectual history—what some have called the postmodern era—where a new perspective is available. (It is my contention that there are different kinds of postmodernism and that not all of these are faulty. One form of postmodernism is based on the understanding that we are now able to critique the more recent past more realistically than previously). From the perspective given to us currently, the modern era can be understood more clearly. According to the philosopher Hans-Georg Gadamer, we now understand how the anti-tradition prejudices of the Enlightenment forestructured the modern understanding of reality and prejudiced moderns to interpret the world as they have. It is a world devoid of the mystery of the sacred because of an overarching postulate that the dimension of the sacred does not and cannot exist. Or, to express this in other language, we have been tutored by the modern secular imagination to see the world merely as a world of raw fact which symbolizes nothing beyond itself. This causes many people to put arbitrary limits on what is possible at the hand of God.

A thorough examination of modern intellectual prejudices and an analysis of why moderns prefer some answers over others—indeed, why some moderns prefer certain questions over others—goes a long way to deliver the interpretive imagination from its enthrallment to the regnant dark aspects of Enlightenment or modernist ideology. (Not everything associated with the Enlightenment, it is pointed out, is negative. There are both bright and dark sides of this period in Western civilization). A postmodern critique of the modern secular imagination and its theoretical underpinnings tends to free the imagination to the truth that all is possible with God. Postmodernism, according to the view expressed here, involves not only a critique of the modern but also a retrieval of the classic. This does not suggest that premodern ideals are to be restored to throne in all of their glory, but it does advise that the Christian imagination must return to its classical roots in every age.

The fifth and final chapter, "The Risen Christ Today," reviews briefly what some prominent Biblical scholars have written about the resurrection of Jesus in recent years. The chapter also describes Jesus in the framework of First Corinthians as being *really present* in human history today via the modes of presence in Church, presence in Biblical word, and presence in the Lord's Supper or Eucharist. Jesus has risen, it is claimed, into the glory of his Father and also into Church, Biblical Word, and Sacrament. Analysis of the concept of real presence is undertaken to show that the real presence of Jesus in the world today is not unacceptable to an interpretive imagination that has been released from the confinement imposed by modernist secular ideologies. The Christian message of the resurrection, *enacted* by contemporary followers of Christ, has a liberating effect on the human imagination today in Church, Biblical Word, and Sacrament. This is the resurrected body which confronts the peoples of the world as a summons to faith.

It is possible today to affirm Jesus as risen, despite the influence of the modern secular imagination, because of the intuitional prompts from the collective unconscious (the resurrection meaning structure) and the gift of faith which makes it possible to interpret something imaginatively as something else, e.g., the Church as presence of the resurrected Jesus.

Finally, it is maintained that the resurrection of Jesus was not promulgated by the apostles as an intellectual conundrum but as the all-surpassing saving deed in human history of the God who acts in history. As such the heralding of the resurrection of Jesus is not an issue to be debated but instead an event that is normative for all discourse concerning ultimate meanings. In the resurrection, God is revealed again as the God of history. Far from being the god of deism, the God beyond all gods is the God who is closer than we can presently imagine. He is particularly present in the people of God who witness from east to west the works of his power and love, in the dynamism of the Biblical Word, and in Sacrament. His presence in these particular modes of presence, however, does not exhaust the modalities of his presence.

Appendix A presents a concluding reflection on the construction of pagan resurrection myths. Those who created these myths, I hypothesize, possessed an intuitive understanding of the resurrectional structure of the created world, a sense of the resurrection meaning structure inherent in the profound reaches of the psyche, and were familiar with what Joseph Campbell would later call the great monomyth, the story of a hero who went out from the community into a dangerous situation only to return again full of gifts for the members of the community. Pagan resurrection myths were devised over a long period and eventually communicated insights into the structure of the world on behalf of its Creator. Pagan resurrection myths, then, were in some sense revelatory.

Appendix B looks at the resurrection in respect to language and the meanings that attach to the notions of "body" and "matter" in respect to the bodily resurrection of Jesus. The common notion of "body" does not do justice to the complex meanings associated with the term as it is used in respect to Jesus' resurrection..

Several persons evaluated the initial manuscripts. I wish to thank Mary Margaret Funk, OSB, for her wide-ranging assessment of the text. Her comments on the importance of the religious imagination, among other observations, were extremely valuable in my rewrites of the manuscript. Matt Hayes offered numerous suggestions that assisted in the improvement of the manuscript in many respects. His sensitivity to the nuances of some of my statements in the original manuscript was beneficial to the entire thrust of the finished product. He also showed me a need for documentation that was lacking in the initial draft. Joseph Martos read the manuscript with a professor's eye for salient detail. He helped me gain good insights into several points. Chief among these was my evaluation of the Enlightenment. I hope the view of the Enlightenment expressed in the following pages is balanced and evenhanded. R. Michael Harton evaluated the manuscript from the standpoint of Evangelical theology. His comments helped me understand some things that complemented the largely Roman Catholic concepts I brought to the work as a writer. In my experience, Evangelical Protestants and Roman Catholics seem to be largely in harmony on their understandings of the resurrection. His observations were worthwhile in many ways and provided another dimension to the book. Gerard Weber brought me to the understanding that the present work is aimed less at persons in the pews and more toward scholars and those who may be wrestling intellectually with the question of Jesus' resurrection. Dan Mulhall brought to my attention that my claim of the appropriateness of Jesus' resurrection is rooted in the theological notion of grace building on nature, i.e., of course the human soul is naturally Christian (*Anima Christiana naturalitur est*) because God is the creator as well as the savior and sanctifier of the human soul. It is sometimes surprising how helpful a few brief comments can be. To all of the above I extend my gratitude. None of above, of course, must be held responsible for any shortcomings in the work. Every writer sometimes ignores advice for one reason or another. I confess I did not always follow the advice I was offered and, therefore, take full responsibility for what is lacking in the following pages.

I wish to dedicate this book to the memory of someone who was both a scholar of the Bible and an effective teacher. He opened new vistas of understanding for his students almost every time he opened his mouth, and sometimes when he was completely silent. Bruce Vawter, a Vincentian priest who taught at Kenrick Seminary in St. Louis, St. Thomas Seminary in Denver, DePaul University in Chicago, and in workshops across the country, will be remembered by the hundreds of his students who did not reckon, perhaps, what good things were happening to them as they sat thoughtfully in his classes.

Leon McKenzie
Greenwood, Indiana 1996

1

QUESTIONING THE REALITY OF
THE RESURRECTION OF JESUS

Denial of the bodily resurrection of Jesus, at one time the preoccu-
pation of an intellectual elite schooled in anti-religious ideology and
largely unschooled village atheists, is now the argument, amazingly, of many
who call themselves Christian. Almost all of these denials in some way
associate Jesus' resurrection with pagan resurrection myths. Simply put,
usually the argument is that Jesus' resurrection is "nothing but" another
myth in a long line of myths.

The word myth, of course, is used in a largely pejorative sense: A resurrection myth expresses an esoteric speculative doctrine in story form.
The myth holds some merit in that the story line ordinarily carries some
kind of moral or lesson. Beyond this the myth does not refer to actual
events. Resurrection myths are ahistorical. They do not depict actual
occurrences since it is assumed no one can rise from the dead. At most,
resurrection myths contain symbols that always point to transcendental
values but never to actual facts.

Chapter Outline

The burden of this chapter is fourfold. First, three relatively recent
books are examined briefly to document the growing tendency on the
part of writers to dismiss the resurrection of Jesus as mythical in the sense
noted in the previous paragraphs. Second, the concise critical reviews of
these books is followed by an analysis of the model of Biblical-historical
research that is sometimes associated with the rejection of Jesus' resur-

rection. That is, a general answer is provided for the question "Under what research conditions or methods of procedure do individuals, including Christians, produce books that reject the bodily resurrection of Jesus?" Third, a short inquiry into the distinction between the Jesus of history and the Christ of faith is discussed. This distinction occasionally frames historical research about Jesus in such a manner that the dismissal of the resurrection is the only allowable conclusion. Finally, the chapter concludes with some observations about Sir James Frazer's *The Golden Bough*, a classic and influential work that documented the myths of dying and reviving gods. *The Golden Bough* is sometimes cited as a source book that supports the notion that the resurrection of Jesus is "just another myth."

Three Books: Repudiations of the Resurrection

The three relatively recent books that support the rejection of Jesus' resurrection have enjoyed a measure of popular success. This is unfortunate because each of the books is seriously flawed. The first book was written by the Englishman A.N. Wilson, a celebrated biographer. The second author is Barbara Thiering, an Australian who teaches at Sydney University. She is described on the back cover of the paperback edition of her book as "a renegade scholar." The third book was written by John Shelby Spong, an Episcopal bishop and noted activist who supports so-called progressive causes. Each of these writers takes a different tack in questioning the actual bodily resurrection of Jesus but arrives at similar conclusions about the actual bodily resurrection of Jesus. Together these authors provide an opportunity for critical reflection on the central tenet of Christianity.

Wilson's *Jesus: A Life*[1]

A. N. Wilson is widely honored as a biographer for his books on C.S. Lewis, Milton, Belloc, and Tolstoy. Each of Wilson's biographical subjects, it should be noted, was associated prominently with religion. It is quite possible, in the light of what Wilson tells us about himself in his books, that he embarked on the study of these men's lives for the purpose of working out his own search for God. This is not unusual for many writers who harbor unanswered religious questions and dilemmas.

Previous to his book about Jesus, Wilson wrote *How Can We Know?*, a 1985 book that asks how much of the Christian religion is true and how much is a modern Christian obliged to admit is false "now that the atheists have won."[2] In the end, the author argues that what is unknowable is not necessarily unbelievable. My initial thought when I read the book was not that it was a defense of religious faith as it purported to be. My first judgment was that the author seemed to be undergoing a crisis of faith, and interior struggle of great moment. I read the book is a *cri de coeur*, a plea for someone to provide for the author an iron-clad argument that God exists and a proof that Jesus is God's man in human history. Wilson, in both books, appears to be a 19th century rationalist for whom Reason—always spelled with an upper case R by sturdy rationalists—is the final arbiter of the most important matters in life, notwithstanding the fact he concludes *How Can We Know?* with St. Augustine's insightful prayer to God: "Thou hast created us for thyself, and our heart cannot be quieted, till it may find repose in thee."[3] Perhaps he is yet a 19th century rationalist who is working through important questions in his life.

Wilson confesses that as a youth he was very impressionable and very enthusiastic about many things. He became, in turn, a convert to a "simple sort" of evangelical Christianity, an atheist, and a Marxist with strong leanings to the teachings of Chairman Mao. He was also, briefly, a Roman Catholic. His restlessness, perhaps, remains even after *Jesus: A Life*. Perhaps his rejection of the resurrection of Jesus will not deliver him from a need to reconsider the issue in the future. Quite often these matters arise again in consciousness even though they have been dismissed by what one believes is Autonomous Reason.

The author is honest enough to admit in the preface of the book that his actual methodology is "sadly illogical" and that anything we say about the historical Jesus must begin with the word "perhaps." He also concedes that every interpreter of Jesus begins with prejudice. Unbelievers, he observes, as well as those who believe in Jesus create a Jesus in their own image. This is an important insight, an insight not always recognized nor acknowledged by searchers for the historical Jesus.

Wilson claims that his work is not a spiritual autobiography and that his interpretation of Jesus is dispassionate. On both of these counts, I would argue, he is mistaken. He throws himself into the attack against Christianity with vigor and intensity. Sometimes his enthusiasm for pressing his case gets in the way of his objective to show Christianity as a mere human invention.

His case against Christianity is sometimes flawed, despite the fervor of his argument, by inaccuracy and even superficiality. For example, he writes that Paul's teaching on grace could almost be called a theological invention "if one could be totally sure that it owed nothing to Jesus himself."[4] The notion of God's grace, his benevolent and unmerited favor toward his creatures, is a concept that originated in the Hebrew Testament. It would be more accurate to state that Paul re-interpreted the notion of God's loving-kindness in the light of Jesus Christ, i.e., that Jesus is God's sign of his benevolent favor in human history. The statement that Paul could have invented the notion of grace is baldly erroneous.

Likewise, it is difficult to understand why Wilson puts non-canonical gnostic documents such as the gospel of Thomas and the book of James on the same footing as the canonical gospels. The canonical gospels are based on early oral traditions, liturgical practices, and written remembrances of Jesus; these gospels were deemed to be within the scope of orthodoxy. The canonical gospels evidence a discernible historical core. Gnostic documents, on the other hand, are generally founded on esoteric tenets, and tend toward a sense of the magical and abstract wisdom. On their face they appear eccentric even in translation. Wilson's rejection of the Christian interpretation of Jesus is based to a degree on these apocryphal works that were excluded from the New Testament canon. For example, the canonical gospels reveal almost nothing about the childhood of Jesus. Wilson cites the apocryphal gospel of Thomas and relates a story about Jesus at age five. He made birds of clay on the Sabbath. When others remonstrated, Jesus clapped his hands and the birds flew away. Is the silliness of this story supposed to redound to the shame of the Christian faith today? Are we expected to throw away the canonical gospels because this foolish story appears in the apocryphal literature disowned by the Church? It is almost as if Wilson decided to use any kind of ammunition against orthodox Christian belief, even ammunition that has no explosive force.

A final example closer to the theme of this chapter: Wilson employs the word resurrection in an ambiguous sense when he discusses, on the one hand, the resurrection of Jesus and, on the other hand, the resuscitations of Jairus' daughter (Mark 8:40ff), Lazarus at Bethany (John 11:11ff), and the son of the widow of Naim (Luke 7:11ff). There is absolutely no parity between the resurrection of Jesus as presented in the gospels and the reanimation of those revived by Jesus, although stories of those reanimated by Jesus point to Jesus' coming victory over death. Jesus rose to a new life completely different from human life as we know it; those revived by Jesus awakened to continue their lives where their lives were interrupted. Wilson includes among these so-called resurrected individuals those mentioned in Matthew 27: 52-53. After the death of Jesus "the tombs also were opened, and many bodies of the saints who had fallen asleep were raised. After his resurrection they came out of the tombs and entered the holy city and appeared to many."[5] Somewhat flippantly the author asks whether these persons ascended to heaven or whether they had their dying to do over again. If Wilson did not detect the difference between Jesus resurrection and the other so-called resurrections from the internal evidence of the text, he lacked even an ordinary critical sense. If he did detect the difference and proceeded to make a debater's point, he lacked even an ordinary sincerity in expressing himself so frivolously.

In his interpretation of the resurrection of Jesus, Wilson "guesses" that the followers of Jesus "had actually seen James, or another of the brothers of the Lord. The angels or young men who told the women that he had 'gone before them into Galilee' were members of Jesus' family, who had come in the garden tomb in order to take the body for burial near his home in Nazareth."[6] There is not the slightest scrap of evidence to support these "guesses." Wilson's conjectures are undiluted speculations.

Wilson: Jesus and Pagan Mythology

The real villain in the piece, according to Wilson, was Paul. As the "inventor of Christianity" Paul commends Jesus "in purely mythological terms. Jesus is the Messiah; Jesus is the Rock in the desert from which the people of Israel drink pure water; Jesus, like Mithras, God of the Morning, can be drunk from an uplifted cup of blood: Jesus, the dying demigod who comes to life again, is the conqueror of death itself."[7]

In his missionary activity, Paul needed to address both the Jews in the diaspora and the Greeks. Once he implanted the "essentially Jewish Messianic idea into alien Gentile soil, the Gentiles would have difficulty in turning Jesus into a God; and not merely Jesus, of course, but also Paul, and the Caesars, and anyone else whom they happened to admire."[8] In the polytheistic mission field, it was not surprising that Sts. Paul and Barnabas, preaching in Lycaonia, were mistaken for divine beings. It was not at all surprising, according to Wilson, that the Jewish Messiah would be thought of in divine terms; it was not at all surprising that Jesus would have been interpreted as a God. St. Paul made the most of pagan myths and expectations by pointing to Jesus as the Messiah and as a divine being who redeemed us from sin and promised everlasting life.

After reading Wilson's treatment of Jesus, I was not at all moved by his arguments. I did gain the impression, though, that A. N. Wilson is not totally comfortable with his interpretation of Jesus. Wilson has taken a common and shop-worn argument against Christianity, i.e., that Paul of Tarsus is the true inventor of Christianity, and has built his entire understanding of Jesus around this scenario. Once Wilson overcomes the tired rationalism that now possesses him, once he recognizes there is no absolutely convincing argument or fail-safe formula for proving or disproving that Jesus was raised by his Father from the dead, he may reconsider his position. He must first, however, learn to deal with intellectual complexities more handily, at a deeper level of analysis, and more honestly.

Thiering's *Jesus and the Riddle of the Dead Sea Scrolls*[9]

A blurb on the cover of the paperback edition of Barbara Thiering's *Jesus and the Riddle of the Dead Sea Scrolls* informs the prospective reader that Thiering is a Biblical scholar, theologian, and Dead Sea scroll expert. The blurb continues to state that the author presents a "whole new picture of the origins of Christianity and the identity of Jesus." To wit, Jesus was not born in Bethlehem but into a royal priestly line of a strict sect at Qumran, the site of the finds of the Dead Sea scrolls. He was born out of wedlock to a betrothed "virgin" woman. He did not die on the cross but was drugged and later revived in a burial cave. He was married twice and fathered three children. As an outcast he befriended the poor, the sick, women, and gentiles, and rejected the legalism of his sect. He performed no miracles.[10]

How did Thiering discover these things? The New Testament was written in a code which the author deciphered, she claims, by means of a new method of reading the gospels. The *pesher* method (*pesher* is Hebrew for interpretation) entails reading a text and then applying what was written in ages past to the current situation. Thiering maintains she cracked the code of the gospels thereby enabling her to read the subtext beyond the text originally intended by the author. Basing much of her research on gnostic texts and Essene documents, Thiering arrives at veritably stupendous conclusions.

First, Jesus did not die on the cross but overcame the effects of poison, escaped from the tomb, and stayed with friends until he reached Rome where he lived until 64 A.D. Second, the hill of the skull was not located in or near Jerusalem but at the site of the Qumran buildings. Further, Jesus was not hung on the central of the three crosses, but on the western-most cross of the three. Third, the "account of the marriage of Jesus with Mary Magdalene lies very close to the surface of the gospel narrative. It is easy to sense an erotic element in the story of the woman with the alabaster flask of pure nard who poured it over Jesus.[11]

Fourth, the three leading Jewish priests at the time during which a branch of Judaism was transformed into Christianity were called Father, Son, and Spirit.[12] A final amazing example of the pesher technique as employed by Thiering: When the second son of Jesus was born in 43 A.D. this event was coded in the Acts of Apostles in 12: 24 as "the Word of God increased." At this time in his life Jesus, according to the author, was known as "Word of God."[13]

Thiering proposes "Rules for the Pesharist" and requires at the beginning of these rules that new habits of interpretation need to be worked out by modern readers of the gospels. What the rules suggest to me is an elaborate justification for the unconstrained exercise of one's imagination anent textual materials. A complicated chronology of alleged events, a description of the locations at which these events occurred, and an appendix describing the hierarchy of persons involved in the events are also presented. One of the insights of the author in the discussion of the hierarch of persons in the gospels is that "The Many" and "the crowds" were actually only one man who represented a large group of people. The Rules for the Pesharist and other appendices are largely sophistical. They take on the surface appearance of serious scholarship but are densely obtuse for anyone unfamiliar with Biblical hermeneutics.

No doubt deconstructionists involved in literary criticism in some American universities who recognize the text of any composition as indeterminate—with the result the text is open to any meaning assigned by the reader—would find no difficulty describing Thiering as a scholar.[14] Anyone who would write, however, that throughout "Christian history, the resurrection has not been treated as the very pivot of faith" and that emphasis on the resurrection "is something that has developed in recent times"[15] is simply out of touch with Biblical texts, church history, and historical theology. N.T. Wright, a New Testament scholar of international standing, wrote that Thiering's comments about the recency of the importance of the resurrection for Christian belief "is one of the most extraordinary statements in this bizarre book."[16] What is operative in Thiering's book, I suggest, is not scholarship but overwrought fancy. The content of the book is gauged essentially to titillate readers and not to enlighten.

Thiering: Pagan Myth and Jesus' Resurrection

According to Thiering, early Christians who were astute explained the resurrection of Jesus in terms of myth for "babes in Christ" or those who were slow or otherwise immature. There were those who were "in" on the information that Jesus did not die on the cross and those who were irredeemably naive. The tale of Jesus' resurrection from the dead was propagated by someone who understood the need of naive Christians for myth. This was, remarkably, Simon Magus. Later, other Christians who opposed Simon Magus felt a deep need to record the truth without destroying the faith of the weak in the resurrection. They wrote the gospels and Acts, therefore, in a code. On the surface, simple Christians could read the myth. Those who knew better could use the pesher method to read the hidden subtext and to understand what really happened. All of this is redolent of a gnosticism wherein the initiates possess knowledge and crafts not available to those who are not introduced to the mysteries of the cult.

Commenting on the virgin birth of Jesus, Thiering states that the new "Judaeo-Christian religion coming to the pagans had to compete with such cults, and Christians found the circumstances of Jesus' conception an ideal basis for a deliberately constructed myth.[17] Given that the use of the persher method disclosed to Thiering that Jesus did not rise from the dead, the myth of the resurrection was obviously another deliberately constructed myth for missionary purposes to attract pagans to Christianity.

One wonders at the extent some writers will go to attract attention, gain an audience, and sell books. Some Biblical-historical research is based on surmises, scholarly or otherwise. Other Biblical-historical research is tainted with the psychological eccentricities of writers who blend scholarly competence with extremist views that are just clever enough to pass for progressive. Perhaps the largest lesson to be learned from such writers is that not everyone who has an academic title or advanced degree is an authentic scholar. Lay persons should never become so impressed by a celebrated writer that they fail to question critically what the writer says and writes.

Spong's Resurrection: Myth or Fact?[18]

John Shelby Spong is the Episcopal bishop of Newark. As a leading figure in various social movements—including the ordination of an active homosexual to the Episcopal priesthood—Spong is no stranger to controversy. Nearly everything he touches, it seems, attracts the lightening of criticism. Spong's book *Resurrection: Myth or Fact?* is another example of his espousal of positions that provoke notoriety.

The key to his interpretation of the historical Jesus and what "really happened" regarding the resurrection of Jesus is Spong's use of the concept of midrash. The sense of midrash is "to interpret" or "to explicate" Biblical passages. The entirety of Chapter One of Spong's book is devoted to the celebration of the freeing use of midrash as the concept is understood by the author. No one, avers Spong, can hope to understand the New Testament without midrash as the dominant interpretive paradigm.

Midrash, Spong writes, "is the Jewish way of saying that everything to be venerated in the present must somehow be connected to a sacred moment in the past."[19] This is one aspect of midrash that is verifiable: To the pious Jew, what is sacred or conceived as an authentic divine action in the present must have continuity with the tradition of God's saving deeds in history. To interpret any present event as coming from God it is necessary to connect that event with the past events in which God revealed himself. These past events constitute the process of salvation history within which God saves his people and reveals himself. So far, so good.

Spong maintains that much of the New Testament is essentially midrashic writing, that is, Hebrew Testament images were woven together to dramatize the memory of Jesus of Nazareth. Thus, the account of Jesus feeding the multitudes (Mark 6:30-44, Matthew 14: 13-21, Luke 9:10-17, and John 6:1-14) is a story constructed to show Jesus as the New Moses who feeds the people in the wilderness. Midrash, states Spong, is "a way to think mythologically about dimensions of reality for which the language of time and space were simply not appropriate."[20] In other words, whether Jesus actually fed the multitudes does not matter, what matters is that the memory that Jesus is the New Moses was incorporated into the religious tradition.

Two comments regarding Spong's references to midrash must be expressed at this point. First, it seems that Spong has not grasped the concept of midrash adequately. Midrash may be either a process of interpretation or an artifact which results from the process. As artifact midrash could take any of multiple forms. The chief of these formats are: 1) a verse-by-verse exposition of scripture, 2) a homily that elaborates the meaning of a scripture passage in question, or 3) a rewritten narrative version of a Biblical passage. Midrashim may be classed in terms of a number of literary genres. Hallachic midrashim refer to legal matters, haggadic midrashim are of a nonlegal character. In addition, there are exegetical midrashim that are commentaries of Biblical books, homiletical midrashim develop sermon topics, and narrative midrashim present legendary materials associated with Biblical stories.[21] The bishop apparently thinks that most of the gospel writings are edifying tales or legends: narrative fictional accounts of the life of Jesus. His understanding of midrash reduces the concept to a single limited aspect of its overall meaning. That is, he has committed the fallacy of taking the part of something for its whole. He also believes, it seems, that these fictional narratives can be explained and decoded by looking at them through the lens of midrash, a lens that Spong, according to his testimony, has mastered.

Second, the bishop seemingly fell under the spell of the Hammer Effect while writing the book. The late psychologist Abraham Maslow was reputed to have first enunciated the Hammer Effect: "Give a boy a hammer and he will find that everything needs pounding." After he discovered the hammer of midrash, Spong found that most New Testament texts needed pounding. In the New Testament, in Spong's view, an entire world of midrash awaits the explanations of Bishop Spong who holds the key—after nearly two millennia—to the final uncovering of its authentic meanings.

Philip Alexander, in his article "Midrash" in *A Dictionary of Biblical Interpretations,* states that an inaccurate use of the word "is problematic since it runs the risk of evacuating the term of any specific meaning and reducing it to jargon."[22] It seems that Bishop Spong has reduced the term midrash to jargon. The notion is given such a broad definition—"a way to think mythologically about dimensions of reality for which the language of time and space was simply not appropriate"—that Spong allows himself the luxury of running through the New Testament with unfettered imagination to decipher meanings of Biblical passages with an *ex cathedra* ease that astounds more than it illumines.

Prior to his reconstruction of the life and death of Jesus, the author makes the usual disclaimer that his account can be nothing more than speculation. "No one can finally do anything other that speculate."[23] He makes it clear, though, that his speculation is grounded on scholarship. The speculations of writers who reconstruct a Jesus who is at odds with the Jesus of the canonical gospels and with the ongoing tradition of the Church are ordinarily vested in the trappings of scholarship. The bishop's work is a case in point. What he gives with one hand ("This is specula-tion") he takes away with the other ("but it is scholarly speculation"). He merely exemplifies a tactic that has been employed often in the history of reconstructions of the Jesus of history.

In his elaboration of "what really happened" after the death of Jesus, the author views nearly everything as midrash in the sense of edifying tale. This tale is told to avoid the scandal that Jesus' body, after his death, was dumped unceremoniously in a common grave. New Christians in the Greek world would recoil that Jesus, the divine-man, would undergo such a fate. The myth of the bodily resurrection of Jesus was thus invented.

Much of what Spong writes preliminary to his denial of the bodily resurrection of Jesus is well worth reading. He collects the ideas and interpretations of a number of modern scholars. These ideas provide helpful insights into the gospels. As he moves toward his statement repudiating the bodily resurrection of Jesus, however, he moves more and more (it seems) in an eccentric trajectory. His interpretation becomes labored and difficult to accept as realistic, even by someone who accepts that edifying accounts are contained in some places in the gospels. The nativity account of Luke, for example, can very easily be read mistakenly as midrash. Even in these infancy narratives, however, one never knows enough to differentiate between the core facts of the narrative and the embellishments that have been added.[24]

The Resurrection According to Bishop Spong

Here is what Bishop Spong believes about the resurrection of Jesus. A few verses in the Acts of the Apostles, according to Reginald Fuller whose ideas Spong follows, presents a burial tradition concerning Jesus that is different from all others.[25] This different burial tradition can be found in Acts 13:28-31, i.e., in Paul's sermon to the Jews living in Antioch. "Even though they found no cause for a sentence of death, they asked Pilate to have him killed. When they had carried out everything that was written about him, they took him down from the tree and laid him in a tomb. But God raised him from the dead, and for many days he appeared to those who came up with him from Galilee to Jerusalem, and they are his witnesses to the people."

Spong focuses on the phrase "*they* (emphasis mine) took him down from the tree and (*they*) laid him in a tomb." That is, they (those who lived in Jerusalem and their rulers) killed Jesus and buried his body in a com-mon grave. The bishop claims this burial tradition cited in Paul's sermon evidences that Paul himself did not know of any other burial tradition. One may infer, therefore, that other burial traditions involving Joseph of Arimathea, for example, were mere fictional narratives without any foundation in fact. Spong contends that while the Acts of the Apostles was redacted later than the gospels, there is good reason to believe the words of Paul's sermon about Jesus' burial by his killers constitute a primitive formula.[26]

Bishop Spong goes on to base his argument on Five Clues. The first clue locates the resurrection not in Jerusalem but in Galilee. Appearances of the risen Jesus in Jerusalem are mere stories. The second clue addressed the primacy of the apostle Peter in the resurrection account. After the resurrection, it is hypothesized, Peter and the rest of the apostles escaped to Galilee. After grieving a number of months, Peter finally "saw" the meaning of Jesus' life and "saw" that Jesus had been "lifted into the living God. It had nothing to do with empty tombs or feeling wounds. Peter shored up the faith of the other apostles and they also "saw" that "Jesus had made God real and that God had taken the life of Jesus into the divine nature."[27]

The third clue is that the common meal celebrated by Jesus and the apostles prior to his death was an eschatological meal. In later celebrations of the Eucharistic meal in Galilee, Jesus was experienced in the breaking of the bread. The themes of "resurrection, bread, ascension, spirit, and the confession of Peter are the elements that came together at the dawn of Christianity..." Just as the bread was taken, blessed, broken, and given, so also was Jesus. Jesus was the bread of life "for his life has now been lifted into the very life of God."[28]

The fourth clue is that the resurrection did not occur "on the third day" or "three days after" Jesus' death. Spong argues that the phrase "the third day" was, in fact, an eschatological symbol. "Three days" did not indicate chronological time but the decisive revelation of God that was to begin the end times.

Finally, the burial tradition is viewed by the author as mythology. "... the story of Joseph of Arimathea was developed to cover the apostles' pain at the memory of Jesus having had no one to claim his body and of his death as a common criminal. His body was probably dumped unceremoniously into a common grave, the location of which has never been known—then or now."[29]

Later, Jesus was made into a divine-man in the minds of the Gentiles who received the primitive message of the apostles and was portrayed in a fantastical way in the gospels. This transformation of Jesus into a divine-man was undertaken for, and perhaps by, the Gentiles who entered the Church. They received Jesus intellectually and imaginatively into their existing categories of thought and reflection. It is this Jesus, and not the real Jesus, we follow today. The Jesus we follow today, one may conclude, is the godlike visitor from heaven who fits into the categories of pagan mythology that were paradigmatic for Gentiles at that time. Pagan mythology enters into the resurrection proclamation, therefore, at the point the Gentiles received the "good news" that Peter and the other apostles had strongly experienced when they finally gained insight into the meaning of Jesus' life.

To be fair to Spong, while the initial resurrection of Jesus was merely an insight that dawned upon the grieving Peter, and while the body of Jesus was supposedly committed to a common grave, the bishop nonetheless affirms Jesus as his "primary window to God," he affirms the resurrection "which asserts that the essence of Jesus is the essence of the living God," and he affirms life after death "because one who has entered a relationship with God has entered the timelessness of God."[30]

An Assessment

Bishop Spong's lack of an adequate working definition of midrash has been noted above. His argument that Jesus' resurrection consisted initially in some kind of awareness in Peter and the other apostles, and not in the self-manifestation of Jesus to them, is an argument that resembles dozens of other frivolous notions about the resurrection that have been despatched to the intellectual dust bins of history. There are other assessments, however, that must be made at this juncture.

Bishop Spong exhibits a haughty disdain for Catholic and Protestant "literalists" (at least in his compositional style if not in fact) who are at odds with "the unbelieving world of postmodern men and women (that) dismisses most of the content of organized religion as sheer nonsense."[31] The bishop should be reminded that religious truth is not properly measured by a show of hands. At the same time Spong celebrates the intellectual acumen of those he mistakenly (I believe) calls "postmodern" men and women, he characterizes the resurrection belief of his "literalist" intellectual inferiors as belief in "resuscitated bodies that appear and disappear or that finally exit this world in a heavenly ascension."[32] There may be some Christian "literalists" who conceptualize Jesus as a resuscitated corpse. Most Christians who believe in the risen Jesus, the bishop should know, do not believe that Jesus was raised from the dead as a revived corpse. The Jesus who appeared to his apostles and others manifested himself in a spiritual body, an imperishable body (1 Corinthians 15:44 and 15:52); the body such in the sense of the New Testament *soma*, a body that recapitulates and reintegrates the history of a particular self. More than this, the risen Jesus manifested himself as a spirit-body that was at once, paradoxically, *continuous* with the Jesus who died and *discontinuous* with the Jesus who died in that his resurrected body had been exalted (lifted up) by God into the very glory of God as the first-born of the dead. The risen Jesus is risen precisely as a *soma* that largely surpasses our interpretive capacities for understanding since it is a body that is at once earthly and at the same time a body that transcends what we ordinarily understand by the notion of body. The *soma* of the risen Lord is unique and mysterious.

The World of Pagan Myth and Ritual

In each of the three books reviewed above the idea of the influence of the world of pagan myth is prominent. According to Wilson, Thiering, and Spong, the belief of early Christians in the resurrection of Jesus would not have been possible if the world of pagan myth had not existed. The risen Jesus is "nothing but" another myth because pagan resurrection myths abounded in the ancient world at the time of Jesus.

Thomas Sheehan, a philosophy professor, writes that during the first century of Christianity, the Mediterranean world of pagan religion was flooded with ideas from Greek philosophy, Jewish theology, and various mystery cults.People sought salvation through the mystery religions. The rituals of these religions, Sheehan claims, filled a need for a "god who died or disappeared and then either returned to life or in some way shared divine power with the initiates."[33] Sheehan mentions the Greek mystery religions of Demeter, Dionysus and Orpheus, the eastern cults of Isis and Osiris from Egypt, the Phrygian cults of Cybele and Attis, the Syrian cult of Adonis, and the cult of the Persian god Mithras. The author makes the point that these mystery cults influenced the thinking of Jewish Christians just as these Christian gained converts from those who enjoyed membership in pagan cults.

What is missing in Sheehan's observations is a critical consideration of the specific nature of the relationship between pagan resurrection myths and the resurrection of Jesus. Those who deny the actual bodily resurrection of Jesus are beset with a fixed interpretive gaze that permits them to see the resurrection of Jesus only in terms of pagan resurrection myths, a condition I liken to viewing the situation with permanently crossed eyes. *It is quite possible, however, to see pagan resurrection myths in terms of the resurrection of Jesus.* It is quite feasible to interpret the resurrection of Jesus critically as the normative event that bestows legitimacy on whatever hints of truth are embodied in pagan resurrection myths and rituals. This task, of course, is central to this volume. The interpretive understanding that views the risen Jesus as the focal point of even pagan resurrection myths can be stated neither simply nor briefly. The interpretive understanding that views the risen Jesus as "nothing but" another myth is ingrained deeply in the modern way of thinking and can be displaced by a new interpretive horizon only with some degree of difficulty. Before we can begin to establish this new horizon it is necessary to inquire into the model of Biblical-historical research that would not only permit but also invite some scholars to reject the actual bodily resurrection of Jesus. We must ask the question "Why would some individuals, including Christians, be inclined to write books that repudiate the bodily resurrection of Jesus?" The "why?" in this instance does not seek an answer that refers to psychological motivations but instead asks what assumptions and course of thinking can lead easily to a disavowal of the resurrection.

The Modern Model for Biblical-Historical Research

A research model is essentially a system of standards, objectives, and assumptions that guides researchers in the design and execution of research projects. A model for Biblical-historical research directs the activities of the research specialist who studies the Bible and the historical forces that came into play in the writing of the Bible. According to Gerhard Maier the modern model for Biblical-historical research contributes to a situation wherein the Bible is interpreted as if it were any other ancient document. That is, the researcher approaches the Bible without any acceptance of the special character of the Bible; the model of a specifically "modern" empirical sciences produces guidelines for research activities.

Maier refers to a number of scholars who claim the "modern" scientific approach is inappropriate for the study of the Bible. This inappropriateness stems from two sources. First, "modern" models of scientific research follow the principle of Cartesian doubt. Nothing is accepted as certain that admits of any doubt. While Descartes' notion that systematic doubt is *de facto* the starting point for some philosophical and empirical studies, it seems improper to approach the Bible with systematic doubt since it purports to be of divine origin: the word of God written in the words of writers inspired by God. To reject this claim of divine authorship prior to any serious study of the Bible is to begin the study with a resistance to the Bible that may manifest itself, to one degree or another, in the findings and conclusions of the Biblical research.[34]

Second, Maier cites Karl Girgensohn's characterization of the three principles of "modern" science: 1) the principle of the autonomy of human reason which must operate independent of any reliance on divine revelation, 2) the principle of immanent explanation which allows explication of phenomena only in respect to immediate causes and therefore forbids explaining anything in respect to transcendent causes, and 3) the principle of bias in favor of mechanistic-causal explanations of reality which rule out interpretations other than explanations of the materialist-mechanistic variety.[35]

The approaches of "modern" science, when applied strictly to Biblical research, require the researchers to begin in systematic doubt. Everything in the Bible is doubted until it is proven certain by autonomous human reason. It is little wonder that some Biblical scholars dispute nearly all Biblical passages as irrelevant or even as the product of superstitious minds. In their separation of what actually happened historically from fictional narratives or symbolic allusions in the Bible, nothing that purports to have actually happened in the Bible is genuine unless it is proven beyond a reasonable doubt. When the Bible is studied strictly under the rubric of modern science, the Bible is guilty until proven innocent.[36]

It is the attitude or orientation created by the modern ideas of what constitutes critical study that inclines some students of the Bible to search for ways to discredit anything in the Bible that smacks of superstition or magical thinking. Thus, the miracles performed by Jesus in his public ministry are routinely questioned and usually spurned as fanciful creations of the writers or redactors of the Biblical manuscripts. Something as marvelous and extraordinary as a resurrection from the dead (and not merely a resuscitation of a comatose person) is too much for those who suppose they follow the principles of modern science in their dissection of Biblical passages.

It is a mistake—and this is crucially important—to apply the notion of science *univocally* to physics, chemistry, biology, sociology, psychology, educational measurement, Biblical scholarship, and so forth. Such a broad application of a concept across many different research fields is fallacious. Those who are familiar with research theory in the empirical sciences know that "as one moves from the physical sciences through biology and across the broad spectrum of the behavioral sciences ranging from physiological psychology to cultural anthropology, the number of potential causal factors increases, their representation in measures becomes increasingly uncertain, and weak theories abound and compete."[37]

If Biblical scholarship is viewed as scientific, it is necessarily to understand that multiple weak theories will abound within the field due to the complexity of uncontrollable factors involved in the study of the Bible. It is also necessary to separate out research findings from the subjective biases brought to the research project by the investigator.[38] The methods used by Biblical scholars are not the methods of the hard sciences, sometime pretensions to the contrary notwithstanding.

There is a research continuum ranging from the "hard" data of the systematic empirical sciences such as physics, to the "soft" data of the so-called social sciences. At one end of the continuum some research findings support *conclusive* inferences; other research findings support *suggestive* inferences. Still other findings, at the other end of the contiuum, are so mixed with surmises that inferences can be drawn only with many reservations; these are *speculative* inferences. Biblical-historical research, for all of its importance, often yields many conclusions that are simply *suggestive* or *speculative*. Much Biblical-historical research is weak in its conclusions. This is not to say that Biblical-historical research is done poorly or is uncritical. It is simply to note that some kinds of research, *on the basis of the nature of the research process alone*, are not as probative as others.

A great deal of artistry is involved in Biblical interpretation; there is a great deal of scholarly subjectivity that enters into the identification and definition of Biblical research problems. The philosopher Hans-Georg Gadamer has shown that methods are used by individuals all of whom have been prejudiced by the traditions in which they developed intellectually. All of us are prejudiced in the answers we give to questions. More importantly, *our prejudices incline us to prefer some questions over others*. While the tools of Biblical research are important and helpful, it is frivolous to think that these tools are applied by scholars who are devoid of prejudices and assumptions that forestructure their understanding, prejudices and assumptions that may be invisible to the scholars themselves.[39]

The Jesus of History and the Christ of Faith

Closely related to the issue of the use of the "modern" scientific research model in Biblical studies is the distinction between the Jesus of history and the Christ of faith. The early 19th century witnessed a number of lives of Jesus written by rationalist theologians. A rationalist theologian may be described here briefly as a theologian whose first allegiance is to autonomous human reason. In evaluating the gospels for information about Jesus, rationalist theologians deny the element of the supernatural in the gospels. Thus according to them, miracles were probably based on memories of Jesus but the disciples were mistaken in ascribing these events to anything other than natural causes. Rationalist Biblical scholars would never admit that healings described in the Bible were attributable to divine action.

One of the most important rationalist lives of Jesus was written by D.F. Strauss who argued that the supernaturalist views of the gospels were erroneous. He admitted, however, the value of the gospels as presenting religious myths. Jesus did not rise from the dead, according to Strauss, but was interpreted as risen from the dead by the apostles. Strauss saw very little of historical value in the gospels. In reviewing the efforts of these theologians and others, the theologian Martin Kahler argued that the focus of the Church must be the Christ of faith, the Christ that has been heralded by the Church as risen Lord. Attempts to describe the Jesus of history, the Jesus laid bare from all theological speculation, was fruitless. This verdict did not stop what became known as the quest for the historical Jesus.[40]

The historical Jesus is the "earthly Jesus as known through 'purely' historical research without recourse to faith."[41] While it is possible to learn something of the historical background of Jesus and the conditions in which he lived—all of which is valuable information—it is questionable in my view that we can obtain the purely objectively historical portrait of Jesus sought by most of the rationalist theologians of the 19th century. The distinction between the Christ of faith and the historical Jesus— aside from being dubiously legitimate—has been the occasion of many portraits of the historical Jesus that bear an uncanny resemblance to the authors who drew the portraits. Amazingly, the ideology of the histori-cal Jesus invariably reflects the ideology of the scholar who depicts the historical Jesus.[42] This occurs because the distinction between the Jesus of history and the Christ of faith can mean anything a particular author wants it to mean. Hans Kung many years ago wrote that the frontier between the Christ of faith and the historical Jesus "is particularly hard to define between historical happenings and interpretation of history, between historical account and theological reflection, (and) between pre-paschal sayings and post-paschal knowledge."[43]

The distinction between the Christ of faith and the Jesus of history is problematic and limiting because of the principal operating assumption that derives from the distinction itself. Whatever is written in the canonical gospels can be presumed to be irrelevant to the Jesus of history because the criteria for historical evidence is often set arbitrarily (and sometimes capriciously) by scholars who quest after the historical Jesus. The gospels, it is sometimes maintained, are confessional statements or theological statements of believers and not exact history. All constructions of the Jesus of history, it is held by some, must be *dissimilar* to the gospels to qualify for history.

Those who posit the distinction between the Jesus of history and the Christ of faith, I suggest, must be prepared to state what is given and what is taken away vis-a-vis "rules of evidence" prior to beginning their work. If a "limitations of the study" statement was required up front from Bibli-cal scholars, we might well find that the most important valid evidence relating to the Jesus of history is excluded *a priori* as too confessional or included without sufficient reason for the purpose of advancing the scholar's theological/philosophical agenda. In other words, those who base their work on the distinction between the Jesus of history and the Christ of faith must propose an argument prior to the study that delin-eates precisely what they mean by the distinction and exactly why some evidences in the canonical gospels do not meet their criteria of adequacy for historical evidences. More simply put, this murky distinction between the Jesus of history and the Christ of faith is so obscure and ambiguous it should not serve as a cardinal element in Biblical research. A central part of the problem associated with separating the Jesus of history from the Christ of faith is that there is much confusion about what is meant by "history" and "historical knowledge." Luke Timothy Johnson in *The Real Jesus: The Misguided Quest for the Historical Jesus and the Truth of the Traditional Gospels* eloquently delineates the problems involved in determining a satisfactory interpretive understanding of these two concepts, notions that are essential to any distinction between the Jesus of history and the Christ of faith.[44]

The authors of the books reviewed above developed their ideas, overtly or implicitly, on the basis of the distinction between the Jesus of history and the Christ of faith. This allowed them to pick elements from the gospels that are "unhistorical" with a wilfulness and lack of rigor that ineluctably led to their rejection of the bodily resurrection of Jesus. Given the ambiguity of the distinction between the Jesus of history and the Christ of faith, one can arrive at whatever conclusions one chooses merely by accommodating the meaning of the distinction to one's purposes. The three writers who deny the bodily resurrection of Jesus do so, then, on the basis of the research model they select and the construction they put upon the distinction between the Jesus of history and Christ of faith.

Frazer's The Golden Bough [45]

I learned of the content of Sir James Frazer's *The Golden Bough* many years ago from a fellow traveler during a train ride. Our conversation drifted to the topic of religion and thence to Christianity. He observed that modern scholars had shown the resurrection of Jesus did not really occur. Pagan myths were in the minds of the people of Jesus' time. After Jesus' death his followers experienced visions and proclaimed him risen from the dead. Jesus was nothing more and nothing less than a mythic figure like Adonis, Attis, Osiris, or Dionysus. In final analysis, Christianity was an amalgamation of several resurrection myths that were central to pagan belief for hundreds, perhaps thousands, of years.

I was at a loss to defend my religious beliefs. My partner in the conversation was much older than I and was certainly better informed. I could not engage in an intelligent discussion of pagan resurrection myths due to a lack of knowledge. In any event, my faith in the resurrection of Jesus was based on the living testimony of the Church and not on philosophical speculation. My faith was grounded upon the testimony of a living tradition that extended, I believed, back to the apostles.

The man with whom I conversed appeared to be a kind man, someone who was concerned that a young man such as myself was so naive about religious matters. He advised I would do well to read Sir James Frazer's *The Golden Bough*. The chapter "Dying and Reviving Gods," he said, was particularly revealing. I thanked him for his advice and turned the discussion to baseball.

I had read references to Frazer's work in college texts and numerous other books about religion but had never read *The Golden Bough*. It was not until several years later that I accidently came upon the work in the library. I located the volume that contained "Dying and Reviving Gods" and read with much interest. The author began the chapter with an introduction concerning the changes in nature, transformations that must have impressed ancient peoples tremendously. These people were curious, Frazer wrote, about the changes that each year stripped nature bare and brought it to a death of sorts, thereby menacing human life also. These ancient peoples eventually attempted to take control of nature by magic arts and, later on, by religious theory and practice.

Cyclic changes in nature, particularly the changes that affected vegetation, were eventually attributed to divine powers. By engaging in certain rituals the people thought they could lend assistance to the vegetation god whose failing strength was responsible for the gradual decay of crops. Ceremonies were performed to enable the god to arise from the dead to a new life, and to bring this new life to the votaries of the god. If, after all, the god regained his strength and brought life in the Spring to plants and animals, this god could also bring life in terms of fertility and reproductive success to the god's devotees. It might also be possible for the god eventually to conquer the specter of death that haunted all mortal beings.

I learned much about various gods from reading *The Golden Bough*. I became familiar with the myths that depicted: 1) the Babylonian Tammuz who was the lover of the goddess Ishtar, 2) Adonis who was worshiped in Babylonia, Syria, and by the Greeks, and other localities, 3) Attis, a god worshiped Phrygia by priests who sometimes practiced self-mutilation, 4) various hanged gods including Marsyas, 5) Hyacinth, a god who belongs to Greek mythology, 6) the Egyptian god Osiris, 7) Dionysus or Bacchus, and 8) the goddesses Demeter and Persephone. All of these divinities, according to Frazer, suffered, died, and arose from the dead in pagan resurrection myths.

Frazer seemed to view all of the dying and reviving gods as patterns of Jesus; the cults of these mythic beings were progenitors of Christianity. Several times the author associated pagan mythology directly with contemporary Christian worship. For example, he examined the Good Friday worship practices of Sicilian women who placed newly sprouted plants near effigies of the dead Christ. This occurred "just as the gardens of Adonis were placed on the grave of the dead Adonis... The whole custom—sepulchers as well as plates of sprouting grain—may be nothing but a continuation, under a different name, of the worship of Adonis."[46]

It would be a fair reading of the text, in this place and in others in the book, to suggest that Frazer, at the very least by indirection and intimation, interpreted Christian liturgies and beliefs as little more than pagan myths revisited.

In a later one-volume abridgment of his work, Frazer dropped the "Dying and Reviving Gods" chapter as such and wove his material through several parts of the book with the effect that it sounds less offensive to Christians. According to Theodor Gaster, an editor and commentator in some subsequent editions of *The Golden Bough*, the chapter "Dying and Reviving Gods" was much exploited. This exploitation is evident even today. In a 1993 book David Rich announces that Christianity "was founded on the idea of the seasons—rebirth after winter's death. Dionysus rose from the dead after three days, as did Attis, and became immortal. As with all religions of redemption Christianity features a god who dies and rises again; its followers obtain immortality by oneness with and obedience to the god."[47]

In the section on Demeter and Persephone, Frazer observed that in the face of death all humankind will grasp at straws and will not stop to assess too keenly the arguments for and against the idea of human immortality.

> The reasoning that satisfied St. Paul and has brought comfort to untold thousands of sorrowing Christians, standing by the death bed or the open grave of their loved ones, was good enough to pass muster with ancient pagans, when they too bowed their heads under the burden of grief...and looked forward into the darkness of the unknown. Therefore we do no indignity to the myth of Demeter and Persephone—one of the few myths in which the sunshine and clarity of Greek genius crossed by the shadow and mystery of death—when we trace its origin to some of the most familiar, yet eternally affecting aspects of nature, to the melancholy gloom and decay of autumn and to the freshness, the brightness, and the verdure of spring.[48]

In the above quotation Frazer referenced St. Paul to his words in 1 Corinthians 15:35ff: "But someone will ask, 'How are the dead raised? With what kind of body do they come?' Fool! What you sow does not come to life unless it dies. And as for what you sow, you do not sow the body that is to be, but a bare seed, perhaps of wheat or of some other grain." The dominating concept in Frazer's work treats the suffering, death, and resurrection of gods in the image of the reaping and "death" of food crops in the fall, and the rebirth of these fruits, vegetables, and grains in the spring.

I found the chapter recommended by a chance acquaintance on the train fascinating but hardly the stuff that would seriously challenge the informed faith of most Christians. I did take some pains at the time to analyze the relationship of pagan resurrection myths to the resurrection of Jesus and even wrote up several pages of notes on this relationship. In the press of time, I failed to develop my notes for publication. They have long ago been thrown out, lost, or destroyed. Memory of my insight into the issue, however, always remained in mind and is presented in Chapter Three. There is a way, both plausible and sound, to reverse the contemporary trend of viewing the resurrection in terms of ancient revival myths and to begin appreciating these revival myths as whispered hints of what God would later say, loudly and dramatically, in his decisive revelatory Word uttered in the risen Jesus. To construct this Christian perspective on pagan resurrection myths, of course, it is necessary to begin with a examination of these myths. This investigation, based on *The Golden Bough*, is offered in Chapter Two.

Concluding Remarks

That many writers and shapers of popular opinion, including a bishop of a mainline church, would write to deny the reality of the bodily resurrection of Jesus is probably not a sign, all things considered, that the world is rapidly descending into the depths of unbelief. The arguments posed by A.N. Wilson and Bishop Spong to depict the resurrection of Jesus as purely mythical, in the sense of untrue, are neither new nor vexing to informed Christians. The arguments of Barbara Thiering in her book— characterized by the scholar N.T. Wright as bizarre—may influence large numbers of flighty-minded and uncritical persons but in the long run will be forgotten.

What is more important to understand, I believe, is that many arguments against the bodily resurrection of Jesus are products of the modern age, an age whose foundations were laid in 18th century. In some sense, we have already begun to live in another era that permits us to view the previous era more completely. The notion of postmodernity is graphic but somewhat imprecise. It will do as a descriptor of the present age,

Notes to Chapter 1

1. A. N. Wilson, *Jesus: A Life* (New York: W. W. Norton & Company, 1992).
2. A. N. Wilson, *How Can We Know?* (New York: Doubleday Image Book, 1991), ix.
3. Ibid., 118.
4. Ibid., 33.
5. This gospel pericope, on its face, is of the apocalyptic literary genre and is not meant to be taken in its most obvious literal sense. It is something like a verbal exclamation point to accentuate the momentous character of the death of Jesus. It can also be argued that these verses belong elsewhere and not in the place selected by redactors of Matthew's gospel.
6. Wilson, *Jesus: A Life*, 171.
7. Ibid., 21.
8. Ibid., 19.
9. Barbara Thiering, *Jesus and the Riddle of the Dead Sea Scrolls* (San Francisco: HarperSanFrancisco, 1992).
10. Ibid., back cover.
11. Ibid., 87.
12. Ibid., 339.
13. Ibid., 332-333.
14. "It is probably fair to say that (Jacques) Derrida's thinking has exerted its most radical influence in the Anglo-American world where 'deconstructive criticism' has become almost *de rigueur* in avant-garde circles. The central thrust of such criticism is to dismantle traditional theories of the literary work as a totalised 'book' ...the death of the book founded on the illusion of an original authorial and authoritative truth, heralds the birth of the 'text' as a free play of signifiers open to an infinite number of readings and rereadings." Richard Kearney, "Phenomenology: Jacques Derrida," *Modern Developments in European Philosophy* (Manchester, UK: Manchester University Press, 1986), 123.
15. Thiering, *Jesus and the Riddle of the Dead Sea Scrolls,* 118.
16. N.T. Wright, *Who Was Jesus?* (Grand Rapids: William B. Eerdmans Publishing Company, 1993), 33.
17. Thiering, *Jesus and the Riddle of the Dead Sea Scrolls,* 46.
18. John Shelby Spong, *Resurrection: Myth or Fact?* (New York: HarperCollins Publisher, 1994).
19. Ibid., 8.
20. Ibid., 16.
21. M.P. Miller, "Midrash," in *The Interpreter's Dictionary of the Bible: Supplementary Volume,* ed. Keith Crim, (Nashville: Abingdon, 1976), 593-597. For another explanation of various types of midrash see *The Encyclopedia of Judaism,* ed. Geoffrey Wigoder, (New York: Macmillan, 1989), 487-489.
22. Philip Alexander, "Midrash," in *A Dictionary of Biblical Interpretations,* eds. R. J. Coggins and J. L. Houlden, (London: SCM Press, 1990), 453.
23. Spong, *Resurrection: Myth or Fact?,* 257.
24. The Jewish scholar Geza Vermes gives three examples of gospel midrashim. These are examples of rabbinic interpretation and argument (Mark 7:9-13, Mat-

thew 19:3-8, and Luke 20: 37-38). The examples are not related to the infancy narratives. See Geza Vermes, *The Religion of Jesus the Jew* (Minneapolis: Fortress Publishers, 1993), 66-70. In an earlier work, Vermes refers to the infancy narratives not as midrashim but as theologically motivated stories. See *Jesus the Jew* (New York: Macmillan, 1973), 37.

25. See Reginald Fuller, *The Foundations of the Resurrection Narratives* (New York: Macmillan, 1971), 54.

26. The argument obviously cuts two ways. If the words of Paul's sermon are indeed early and suggest that Paul and others had no knowledge of Joseph of Arimathea, the later burial traditions in the gospels would include details about the Arimathean to set the record straight. There is another alternative interpretation. When Paul referred to those who crucified and buried the body of Jesus, he very likely generalized because it was not his purpose to develop a detailed narrative of the passion and resurrection of Jesus. This would have taken him away from the purpose of his sermon.

27. 27 Spong, *Resurrection: Myth or Fact?*, 257.

28. 28 Ibid., 209.

29. 29 Ibid., 225.

30. Ibid., 292.

31. Ibid., 11. A strong argument can be made that those called "postmodern men and women" by Spong are actually the last representatives of a "modern" era that is disintegrating under withering postmodern criticism. There are some aspects of postmodernism that enable us to evaluate quite clearly the fallacies of the modern era.

32. Ibid., 21. If Bishop Spong did not know that authentic Christian belief does not concern Jesus as resuscitated corpse, he should have known: if he did know that authentic Christian belief maintains Jesus was raised to a glorified body, but chose to speak of the risen Jesus as a resuscitated corpse, he is open to the charge of being supremely disingenuous.

33. Thomas Sheehan, *The First Coming: How the Kingdom of God Became Christianity* (New York: Random House, 1986), 209.

34. Gerhard Maier, *Biblical Hermeneutics*, trans. Robert W. Yarbrough (Wheaton: IL: Crossway Books, 1994), 23-24. Without rejecting the necessity of critical thinking, it is probably more desirable to begin systematic studies not in doubt but in wonder. The primacy of wonder over doubt rests in this: One can wonder that one doubts but cannot doubt that he or she wonders. Wonder opens the mind. Doubt often leads to full-blown skepticism.

35. Ibid., 24. These principles of "modern" science are coming under some scrutiny and refinement today. To some extent, however, they are necessary in physics, biology, and a host of similar scientific endeavors to preserve the criticalness of scientific thinking. When these principles are carried into the so-called "social" and "literary" sciences uncritically, there is a danger of establishing research designs that are inappropriate.

36. This should not be construed, I repeat, as a condemnation of the critical study of the Bible.This criticalness, however, must be kept within certain bounds even to satisfy the criteria of reason. It is fruitless, I suggest, to begin a study of the Bible

without locating it in the religious traditions in which its various books came to be. The Bible cannot legitimately be plucked from these traditions and isolated in a petri dish for clinical study.

37. Jacob Cohen and Patricia Cohen, *Applied Multiple Regression/Correlation Analysis for the Behavioral Sciences* (Hillsdale, NJ: Lawrence Erlbaum Associates, 1975), 7.

38. For a powerful criticism of the assumptions and suppositions of those who "discover" a Jesus who meets the requirements of their own ideologies see Luke T. Johnson's "The Search for the Wrong Jesus," in *Bible Review*, 9, 6, December, 1995, 20-25, 44.

39. See Hans-Georg Gadamer, *Truth and Method*, trans. G. Barden and J. Cumming (New York: Crossroad Publishing Company, 1986), 235-267. I confess to certain of my own prejudices that color the writing of this book. These prejudices are associated with my faith in the bodily resurrection of Jesus, prejudices based on decades of discussion, reading, and reflection. Gadamer would state that only uninformed and unreflected prejudices are threats to personal and scholarly integrity.

40. See John Rogerson, Christopher Rowland, and Barnabas Lindars, *The History of Christian Theology: The Study and Use of the Bible*, ed. Paul Avis, vol. 2, (Grand Rapids: Wm. B. Eerdmans Publishing Co., 1988), 337-341.

41. Gerald O'Collins and Edward Farrugia, *A Concise Dictionary of Theology* (New York: Paulist Press, 1991), 93.

42. One of the most recent quests for the historical Jesus — with the result that the historical Jesus reflects the questor's egalitarian ideology — is John Dominic Crossan's *The Historical Jesus: The Life of a Mediterranean Jewish Peasant* (San Francisco: HarperSanFrancisco, 1991).

43. Hans Kung, *On Being a Christian*, trans. Edward Quinn (New York: Doubleday and Co., 1976), 287.

44. Luke T. Johnson, *The Real Jesus: The Misguided Quest for the Historical Jesus and the Truth of the Traditional Gospels* (San Francisco: Harper, 1996). This slim volume is of tremendous importance in arriving at a solid basis for the intelligent criticism of any quest for the historical Jesus. See especially pages 81-104.

44. James G. Frazer, *The New Golden Bough*, ed. Theodor Gaster (New York: S.G. Phillips, Inc., 1972). Frazer's original work was publishing in 11 volumes in 1890. The work was widely read by scholars and popularized by them.

45. Ibid., 296-297.

46. David Rich, *Myths of the Tribe* (New York: Prometheus Books, 1993), 29.

47. Frazer, *The New Golden Bough,* 366.

48. Ibid., 366. Gaster observes that it is no longer possible "to see in Frazer's 'dying and reviving gods' mere personifications of grain or fruit, or to regard their passion and resurrection allegorising harvest and growth. We now know that in many ancient and primitive cultures, increase and prosperity were thought to be dependent on the presence within a community or locality of a beneficent deity, and that the failure of either or both was regarded as due to his temporary withdrawal

2

DYING AND REVIVING GODS

What is the precise nature of the relationship between pagan myths of renewal and the resurrection of Jesus? No doubt there are similarities between pagan resurrection myths and the gospel narratives of the resurrection, but there are differences as well. To understand the connection between stories of the gods' revivals and Jesus' resurrection, it is necessary to address critically the implications of both the differences and similarities between the two. Some individuals often merely assume that the very idea of Jesus' resurrection is little more than a replay, of sorts, of pagan resurrection myths. The idea and image of resurrection was in the air at the time of Jesus, according to critics of Christianity, and was transferred to the story of Jesus by early Christians who thought in mythological terms and within mythic frameworks. This interpretation, I suggest, is a conspicuous over-simplification and characteristic of those who are unable to grasp neither the subtlety of the issue nor available knowledge about the Bible, myth formation, and the workings of the psyche.

Others argue that the pagan resurrection myths had nothing to do with the proclamation of Jesus' resurrection, either the formulation of the idea of resurrection or the favorable reception of the proclamation of the good news or *kerygma* on the part of Christian converts from Judaism or the Gentile world. To disregard the impact of pagan resurrection myths, on the part of those who proclaimed the Christian message as well as on the part of those who welcomed the Christian message, seems likewise unrealistic. There are similarities between pagan resurrection myths—as these stories are sometimes called—and the heralding of the resurrection of Jesus. To deny these similarities is to close one's eyes in the face of much evidence. It is possible, however, to admit the similarities without becoming trapped in the "nothing but" fallacy, i.e. the story of Jesus' resurrection is nothing but another myth. Not only can the similarities between Jesus' resurrection and pagan resurrection myths be interpreted so as to reject the "nothing but" fallacy, but these affinities can be interpreted to support belief in the reality of the resurrection of Jesus. The universal experience of the resurrection motif in the natural world —the human experience of the themes of death and resurrection—is considered in the next chapter as contributing to the development of meaning structures in the human psyche that facilitate belief in the resurrection of Jesus. In this chapter, however, the differences between the resurrection of Jesus and the resurrections of various pagan deities are spelled out in perhaps greater detail than in many other books. Two pagan cults of the Greco-Roman world—the cults of Dionysus and Mithras—are concisely described with an eye to comparison with the Christian religion. Finally, the differences between early Christian worship and selected pagan mystery religions are also noted. Sometimes it is useful to note not only the cognitive and notional aspects of religions when they are compared and contrasted but also the liturgical aspects. What people do liturgically in the name of their religious commitments is often more revealing than what they say about the nature of their commitments.

Dying Gods: Who Are They?

James Frazer, in the chapter on dying and reviving gods, recounts stories about several gods. These gods are: Tammuz, Adonis, the mother goddess Astarte, Attis, Hyacinth, Osiris, Dionysus, and Demeter and Persephone. He also recounts myths about the burned god and the hanged god.[1] The following summary is based on the subheadings of Frazer's chapter.

Tammuz

Frazer begins his descriptions of dying and reviving gods with a brief observation on the god Tammuz. In Babylonian literature, Tammuz was identified as the young lover of the goddess Ishtar who symbolizes the reproductive powers of the earth. In an obscure tale about Tammuz, it is reported that he died and descended into the nether regions. Ishtar pursued him even into the dark subterranean world. While Ishtar was absent from earth, all passionate love ceased to exist. Humans and beasts alike did not reproduce. Eventually a messenger of the god Ea rescued Ishtar from the land of the dead and with her the god Tammuz. All nature was revived by their appearance.

The death of Tammuz was mourned ritually each year. An effigy of Tammuz was used in the ritual celebration. It was washed, anointed with oil, and clad in a red robe. Tammuz is likened to various quickly fading plants in Babylonian hymns. This ritual commemoration of Tammuz was probably employed as a thanksgiving offering for the revival of nature each year or, perhaps, as a religious-magical performance that assured the revival of nature year after year.

Adonis

Peoples of the Greek world borrowed ideas from the Semitic peoples who worshiped Tammuz. Thus was born the image of the god Adonis. Adonis was a handsome youth who was beloved of Aphrodite, the goddess of love. Aphrodite hid the infant Adonis in a box and gave the box to Persephone, the goddess of the underworld. It was Persephone's task to keep Adonis in her care. When Persephone opened the box and saw the beautiful Adonis, she immediately fell in love with him and refused to give him back to Aphrodite. The goddess of love descended into the depths of the underworld to claim Adonis. The goddesses Aphrodite and Persephone fell into a clamorous dispute which was finally settled by Zeus. He commanded that Adonis must live with Persephone in the nether regions for part of each year and then with Aphrodite in the upper world for the remainder of the year. It was said that Adonis was finally killed by a wild boar. Another mythic tradition has it that Adonis was killed by the god Ares who saw Adonis as a rival for the love of Aphrodite.

Frazer points out that the story of Adonis was ritualized in various ways and in many regions. What was central to the worship of Adonis was ritualized mourning over his death. At Alexandria, for example, images of Aphrodite and Adonis were displayed on couches. Around the figures were fruits of all kinds, cakes, and numerous plants. The marriage of Aphrodite and Adonis was celebrated one day and on the next day women carried an image of the dead Adonis to the ocean where it was committed to the deep. This burial service was accompanied by bitter weeping and mourning.

At Byblus in Phoenicia, the death of Adonis was mourned annually with loud weeping and beating of breasts. Adonis was believed to have died and later to have come to life again and ascended up to heaven.

The devotees of Adonis shaved their heads in mourning. Women who refused to shave their heads were commanded to give themselves over to ritual prostitution with strangers. The wages of their endeavors were dedicated to the shrine of Astarte.

Adonis, according to Frazer, was associated with the rebirth and decay of vegetation. The mourning for Adonis was essentially a mourning rite to propitiate Adonis, the corn-god, who at harvest time was perishing under the sickles of the reapers or was being trod to death under the hoofs of the oxen on the threshing floor.

In this interpretation Adonis is the corn-god who is slain each year and, once propitiated, returns again the following year with his gift of plenty.

Frazer goes on to note what he considers the very close connection between the annual mourning for Adonis and latter-day mourning for the crucified Christ. Thus, the Good Friday ritual celebrations of the crucified Christ, Frazer implies, are little more than the Adonis rituals that have been in vogue for centuries.

Astarte: The Mother Goddess

Aphrodite, Astarte, and Isthar—various names of the great mother goddess of fertility—play a large part in the religious cults of the ancient world. Frazer wrote of the great mother goddess in the context of his chapter on dying gods, it appears, because the great mother goddess played a central role in the stories of the dying gods. These were the goddesses who needed to be implored to assure the birth of children, the growth of livestock, and favorable harvests of fruit and grain. The great mother goddess was a personification of all of the reproductive forces of nature. As we have seen in the myths of Tammuz-Adonis, the handsome god was greatly loved by Aphrodite-Astarte-Isthar. Their sexual union signified the coming together of the energies of the mundane world, a coming together that provoked fruitfulness in this world.

Ritual prostitution—sexual coupling with temple prostitutes within the shrine precincts of the mother goddess—was directly associated with prayers for fecundity. In Cyprus and in other parts of ancient Western Asia, all women prior to their marriage were obliged to prostitute themselves to strangers in the temple of the mother goddess. In these actions the sexual conjunction between Tammuz-Adonis and the mother goddess were "acted out" within the temple as simulations of what would occur between Tammuz-Adonis and the mother goddess thereby assuring the propagation of plants and animals each year. The annual fecundity of the god and goddess became manifest in the rebirth of the Spring season and with this rebirth, the re-establishment of human, animal, and plant life.

The Burned God

Frazer states that a constant feature in the myth of Adonis was the premature and violent death of the god. Various traditions grew up among peoples of different localities as to the death of Adonis. In one local myth Adonis killed himself when he learned of his incest with his daughter. In another tale Adonis lost a musical contest with a god and was put to death by the winner of the contest.

In some places the chief god of the city was burned in effigy. In these places the burning of the straw god probably took the place of an earlier practice of sacrificing a man to the gods. Melquarth, the principal god of Tyre, was said to have burned himself to death. He ascended to heaven in a great cloud amid the peals of thunder. Another variant myth has it that Hercules burned himself to death on Mount Olympus. According to one account, quails were burnt to death each Spring to call forth the resurrection of the vegetation god. Frazer questions whether some Oriental monarchs deliberately burned themselves to death. The circumstances that attended these fiery deaths are not known. Some persons may have committed suicide by burning due to the belief that fire purified, i.e., that fire burned away what was mortal in a person and left only the eternal and spiritual. The spirits of the burned, therefore, were thought by some to survive death somehow and to return to earth to guide humans.

Attis

Attis, according to Frazer, was another of the gods "whose supposed death and resurrection struck deep roots" into the ritual practices of Western Asia. Attis was the Phrygian Adonis. He was a god of vegetation whose death was mourned and whose resurrection was rejoiced over at the Spring festival. According to the myth Attis was beloved of the great mother goddess Cybele. Two accounts of his death are reported. First, Attis was said to have been killed by a boar, like Adonis. Alternatively, Attis mutilated himself (either castration or emasculation) and bled to death. The story of Attis' castration was probably invented to explain why his priests castrated themselves when they entered the service of the goddess Cybele.

The great festival of Cybele and Attis was celebrated at Rome. On the twenty-second day of March a freshly cut pine tree was brought into the temple of Cybele. The tree was greeted as if it were a divinity. It was clothed like a corpse and decked out in wreaths of violets. On the second day of the festival, the Day of Blood, the chief priest cut himself and offered his blood to the tree. Other minor priests and ritual functionaries whipped themselves into a frenzy accompanied by wild music and the clashing of cymbals. They whirled around in circles and cut themselves with knives to bespatter the altar with their blood. All of this was done to honor the god Attis. As the excitement reached its peak, some of the religious novices castrated themselves. The severed members of their bodies, together with the splattered blood, were offered to Attis to allow him to restore his strength for his resurrection.

In another ritual Syrian devotees of Cybele mourned over an effigy of Attis that was later buried. Throughout the period of mourning for Attis, worshipers fasted from bread in imitation of Cybele who also fasted according to the local myth. When night fell, the mourning of the worshipers was transformed to joy at the announcement that Attis had risen from the dead: a sign that the worshipers themselves would rise triumphant from their graves.

On the twenty-fifth of March the rising of Attis was celebrated wildly. The festival became a carnival and universal licence prevailed. Every man and woman did what they pleased to do. The next day was given to rest and relaxation. Secret rites were also held to celebrate the victory of Attis. Information as to the nature of these rites is very limited. Frazer suggests that the rite included a "sacramental meal" and a baptism in blood. A bull was place on a grate and stabbed to death with a spear. Its blood poured through the spaces in the grate and fell upon worshipers below. They exited the pit below the grate covered with the bull's blood. In this ceremony the worshipers were thought to have gained eternal life.

In other places Attis was thought to be a tree spirit who held power over the plants and trees of the earth. Stories of his death and resurrection were interpreted as the ripe grain buried in the granary and coming to life again when it was planted in the ground. A statue of this version of Attis portrays him as covered with ears of corn, fruit in his hand, and a wreath of pomegranates, pine cones, and other fruits on his head. Attis, then, is the one who along with Cybele, the great goddess of fertility, is responsible for the fecundity of the earth. He arises from the dead each Spring to accomplish his wonders in the blooming of fruits, vegetables, and plants, and in the births of animals and humans.

The Hanged God

Frazer begins this section of the chapter with the story of Marsyas, according to some a Phrygian satyr or according to others a herdsman who played the flute. He was a friend of Cybele and roamed the land with her attempting to sooth her grief over the death of Attis. Proud of his ability to play the flute, Marsyas challenged Apollo to a contest. He was vanquished by Apollo and as punishment for his vanity he was flayed alive. Other say he was cut limb from limb. His skin was hung in a cave from which the river Marsyas ran swiftly to join the Maeander river. The flayed god, his skin hung in a cave, thus arose from the dead in the form of a rushing current.

In another myth, men and animals were sacrificed in Upsala by being hung on trees. The victims who were put to death—to the honor of Odin—were either hung or stabbed. Odin was said to have sacrificed himself to himself. He hung on a tree for nine nights wounded with a spear. Odin dedicated his death to himself.

Artemis was hung in effigy annually on a tree in Greece. This seemed to be a representation of a more ancient human sacrifice to Artemis. At Celaenae the tradition that Marsyas was flayed and his skin hung on a tree probably represented a ritual practice of whipping the dead god and hanging his skin on a tree as a method of effecting his resurrection in the revival of vegetation. Tribes in the Phillippines, Mexico, and peoples of the Orient practiced similar rituals.

Hyacinth

The chapter on dying and reviving gods continues with a very brief account of the god Hyacinth. Hyacinth, according to the myth, was the handsome son of king Amyclas of Sparta whose royal seat was at Amyclae. Once Hyacinth was playing quoits with the god Apollo. When he was accidentally struck with one of Apollo's quoits, Hyacinth was immediately killed. Out of sorrow for the loss of his friend, Apollo decreed that out of Hyacinth's blood a flower should grow each Spring to give promise to mortals of a joyful resurrection. The festal day of Hyacinth was celebrated with much gaiety.

Osiris

Osiris was the god of ancient Egypt whose death and resurrection was celebrated annually. He was the most popular of all Egyptian deities and possesses some of the characteristics of Adonis and Attis. The story of Osiris was told by Plutarch.

Osiris was the offspring of the earth-god Geb and the sky-goddess Nut. The sun-god Ra found out about the unfaithfulness of his wife Nut. He decreed that she should be delivered of the child in no year and in no month. Now it happened that Nut had another lover. He was the god Thoth. Thoth played draughts with the moon and won from the moon a 70 second fraction of every day. Thoth compiled five whole days and added them to the Egyptian calendar of 360 days. Thoth's five days, which he gave to Nut, were thus outside of the year of twelve months. Osiris was born on the first of these days outside of the year. On the next four days were born the god Horus, the god Set, the goddess Isis, and the goddess Nephthys. Eventually Set married his sister Nephthys and Osiris married his sister Isis.

Osiris reigned over Egypt and brought the inhabitants out of savagery and cannibalism. He established laws for the Egyptians and taught them to worship the gods. Isis found oats and barley growing wild and taught the people how to cultivate these grains. Osiris taught the people how to grow grapes and make wine. Osiris temporarily handed the government of Egypt over to Isis while he traveled around the world giving all peoples the gifts of cultivation and agriculture. Before he returned home, Osiris was adored by all of the peoples of the world.

Now it happened that Set, the brother of Osiris, plotted against the king. By means of a trick Osiris was entombed in a coffer. The chest was sealed with molten lead and thrown into the Nile. Queen Isis heard of the treachery and wandered up and down attired in mourning robes. On the advice of a god of wisdom, Isis fled to the papyrus swamps of the Nile delta. She conceived a son there while in the form of a hawk and flew above the corpse of her dead husband. The child born of this conjunction was the younger Horus.

The younger Horus eventually fell prey to his wicked uncle Set. Horus was stung by a scorpion and died. Isis asked the sun-god Ra for help. The child-god Horus was delivered from death. In the meanwhile the chest containing the body of Osiris floated down the Nile and out to the sea. Soon it came to the city of Byblus in Syria. At this point the chest that contained Osiris was grasped by the branches of a marvelous tree.

When Isis heard of the fate of her brother-husband Osiris, she went to Byblus and discovered the chest that contained the body of Osiris. She set the chest afire to burn away all that was mortal of him and twittered around in the form of a swallow. The queen of that place, however, put the fire out and kept Osiris from becoming immortal. Finally, Isis took the chest with her, traveled to visit her son Horus at the city of Buto, and hid the coffer containing Osiris.

As the story goes, the wicked Set was out hunting in the vicinity of Buto and found the coffer. He took the body out of the chest and cut it into 14 pieces. This explains why there are many graves of Osiris in Egypt. Isis, however, sailed up and down the Nile and collected the pieces of Osiris' body which she kept safe. After this she buried waxen images of Osiris in many cities. The only part of Osiris not found by Isis, according to Diodorus Siculus, was his penis which was eaten by the fishes. Isis made an image of this body part. This waxen image was used by Egyptians at their festivals.

Isis entrusted the burial of the actual pieces of Osiris's body to the priests. She exhorted them to honor Osiris as a god. Isis also asked that an animal of Egypt be dedicated to the god Osiris. The priests dedicated the sacred bulls Apis and Mnevis to the memory of Osiris and ordered that they be adored as gods because they had helped the growth of agriculture in Egypt.

It came to pass, according to Egyptian accounts which supplement the writings of Plutarch, that when Isis found the corpse of Osiris she and her sister Nephthys lamented his death loudly and long. The mourning rituals of the Egyptians—similar to the rituals for the dead Adonis—became formalized as religious deeds.

The sun-god Ra, paying heed to the lamentations of the two sisters, sent down from heaven the jackal-headed god Anubis who, with the aid of the sisters, pieced together the body of Osiris. They wrapped the body in linen bandages. Isis fanned the wrapped body and, behold, Osiris revived. He became the lord of the underworld and ruler of the dead. He presides at the judgment of the departed whose hearts are weighed in his presence to determine their eternal fates. Frazer concludes the tale by observing that Egyptians saw in the resurrection of Osiris a pledge of their own eternal lives. True to his central thesis, Frazer connects the myth and ritual of Osiris to the agricultural realities of Egypt. Osiris, in Frazer's reading, was both a corn god and a tree spirit.

Dionysus

The god Dionysus, known to the Romans as Bacchus, is the god of the vine, the god of drunkenness and ecstatic behavior. Frazer suggests that

Dionysus found his origin in the rude tribes of Thrace who were given over to drunkenness as a form of worship. Dionysus is the god opposite the god Apollo. Apollo was known for his rationality, order, and moderation; Dionysus was celebrated for his wild abandon, frenzy, and excess. While Dionysus was the god of the vine he was also considered a tree god and was sometimes addressed by his devotees as "Dionysus of the tree." He was also the patron of the ploughman and harvester, and was associated very closely with agriculture and the growth of grain crops.

As to his origin, it is recounted that Zeus took the form of a serpent and had sexual intercourse with the goddess Persephone. She bore him Dionysus, a horned infant. Shortly after his birth Dionysus climbed upon the throne of Zeus and mimicked him by clasping lightning in his tiny hand. Once while Dionysus was gazing upon himself in a mirror, he was attacked by the Titans. He avoided their malice by taking many different forms: the appearance of Zeus himself, a young man, a lion, a horse, and a serpent. Dionysus took the form of a bull and was finally cut to pieces by his enemies. This myth as well as similar stories, in Frazer's opinion, point to an ancient time when the sons of kings were invested with royal dignity and subsequently sacrificed to the gods in place of the father. After his death, according to one tale, the severed limbs of Dionysus were gathered together by Apollo and buried on Parnassus. According to another story, the grave of Dionysus was at Thebes.

In still another account which told that he was born of Zeus and Demeter, his mother pieced him together and he became young again. Other myths state that after his burial he arose from the dead and ascended to heaven. The rituals of Dionysus varied according to different localities. These rituals were usually associated with the sacrifice of animals. The tearing apart and eating of live bulls (and calves) by the worshipers seemed to be a feature of the wild Dionysian rites.

Demeter and Persephone

The myth of Demeter and her mother Persephone, states Frazer, was developed to explain the origin of the Eleusinian mysteries, the most famous of the religious rites of ancient Greece. The Eleusinian mysteries were dramatized as sacred drama on the plain of Eleusis. Demeter was worshiped as the goddess who had given corn to mortals and taught them to sow and cultivate it. Both Demeter and Persephone, then, are associated with, what was to ancient peoples, the mystery of the growth of vegetation.

One day the young Persephone was gathering flowers when the earth broke open and Pluto, the god of the dead, appeared. He snatched Persephone from the earth and carried her away to the subterranean world of the dead. When Persephone did not return home, her mother Demeter became worried and went to search for her. Demeter learned from the Sun that her daughter had been taken captive by Pluto. She hid from the gods and goddesses and, in disguise as an old woman, took up her abode in Eleusis. Since Demeter was responsible for the growth of vegetation, her absence proved dangerous for all mortals on the face of the earth. Demeter would not allow seed to grow until her daughter was restored to her.

The oxen dragged plows in vain and the earth became parched and sterile. Zeus recognized that soon all humankind would die and, consequently, that no sacrifices would be made to the gods. He commanded Pluto to restore Persephone to her mother. Pluto obeyed Zeus' command after negotiating the return of Persephone for four months each year. The remaining eight months Persephone was to be with Demeter in the upper world. All at once the fields bloomed with fruits and vegetables and other plants. The fertility of the land is guaranteed each year because each year Persephone is resurrected from the dead and ascends to the land of the living.

Dying and Reviving Gods: An Assessment

I described in the preceding chapter how the chapter "Dying and Reviving Gods" in James George Frazer's *The Golden Bough* was recommended as appropriate reading for anyone who wished to overcome a naive faith in the resurrection of Jesus. When I read the chapter—and subsequently relevant portions of other volumes in the Frazer collection—my first reaction was disbelief that the stories of dying and resurrected gods could possibly be compared in any serious way to the proclamation of Jesus' resurrection. The differences between pagan renewal myths was such that these myths do not really deserve to be called "resurrection" myths. The resurrection of Jesus was heralded as something dramatically different from the mythic tales of revived gods on at least four counts.

The Resurrection of Jesus and Pagan Heroes

First, it is quite obvious on the face of the account of Jesus' resurrection and the resurrection tales of pagan deities that the former account is rooted in a factual historical context while the latter are essentially fabulous. The testimony of the resurrection of Jesus is substantively different from the legends of the gods that occurred "once upon a time." This is not to say that Jesus' resurrection can be *proven* beyond all possible doubt to be historically objective in the sense there are direct empirical evidences for his resurrection beyond the testimony of his followers. Could a camera have caught the image of the resurrected Jesus? The question cannot be answered without speculation and conjecture. Even then the question may be answered in two ways in the following brief parenthesis.

Parenthesis. From the standpoint of the *subjective experience* of Jesus's resurrection, it is possible a camera could not have registered the risen Lord because a camera cannot see with the eyes of love and faith, nor could a camera enter into the full experience of the risen Jesus. A camera could not commit itself to a personal relationship with the risen Jesus. The resurrection of Jesus was not a bare fact, I propose, without any reference to the faith capacities of those who witnessed the resurrection. Those who completely lacked faith in Jesus two millennia ago probably could not discern the risen Lord then; those who totally lack faith today cannot discern Jesus' presence in, say, his Biblical word or in the "least of his brethren."

On the other hand, from the standpoint of the risen Jesus as *objective bodily presence,* the risen Jesus appeared to witnesses in the sense of an active manifestation or bodily showing on his part. For those who experienced the risen Jesus, the event was apprised by them as factual and objective albeit in a mysterious way. The risen Jesus showed himself not as a specter or ghost, but as an embodied presence; he showed himself simultaneously as one who had been glorified by his Father. He became the first fruits of a new creation. As such the mode of his presence transcended all previous human experience of being bodily present and, therefore, all available language for explaining his mode of presence. Perhaps the risen Jesus could have been captured on film. To conclude this excursus or parenthesis it must be admitted that we do not know what the risen body of Jesus was like.

Suffice it to say here that Jesus suffered and died under Pontius Pilate. Tammuz, Adonis, Attis, and the rest lived "once upon a time" in a fairytale world. The resurrection of Jesus was attested by real witnesses at a precise time in history; the rebirth of various gods occurred in the richly symbolic but perplexing dreams of mythmakers.

In the second place, the witnesses to the resurrection of Jesus did not interpret his resurrection as a renewed divine presence that somehow reinvigorated the fertility of the earth. The resurrected Jesus, in one strand of resurrection appearances, is associated intimately with the breaking of bread and the sharing of the cup, i.e., with the ritual celebration of his sacrifice on the cross (Acts 24: 13ff). This does not imply, however, that the resurrected Jesus was viewed by his followers as a corn-god or tree spirit. It stretches the imagination beyond reason to see in the resurrected Jesus another iteration of archetypal vegetation gods. The Eucharist is a pledge of eternal life, but not in the crude sense of the cyclic return of life referable to the growth of crops, the repletion of livestock, or the restoration of human sexual potency.

Third, while the followers of the resurrected Jesus identified themselves with Jesus in the sacrificial and eschatological meal of the Eucharist, they identified themselves with a real person and not simply a hero construct that arose out of an unconscious mythic archetype. The followers of Jesus saw in him the very fulfillment of Old Testament prophecies. Just as importantly, I argue later, the resurrected Jesus can be viewed as the realization and validation of pagan dreams of resurrection/renewal that were themselves based on archetypal structures of the collective unconscious.

Finally, the resurrection of Jesus produced historical effects that completely overshadowed the historical effects of supposed resurrected pagan gods. Those who preached the "good news" of Jesus' resurrection, as a pledge of eternal life for those who followed after Jesus, turned the world around in an almost miraculously brief span of time. Such a religious revolution did not occur when the followers of various vegetation gods celebrated their causes. Indeed, today no one would waste time arguing whether Tammuz and the other gods actually lived. Tammuz and other gods, as sources of meaning for human history, are non-issues.

Jesus and Pagan Gods: Why the Confusion?

When I completed reading Frazer's book, I understood three things immediately. The use of the term "resurrection" in reference to pagan deities, first of all, exemplified equivocation at its worst. As anyone who read Frazer's book could see immediately, the concepts of death and resurrection as applied to pagan fertility and vegetation gods were in great need of explanation. These concepts do not apply univocally or unambiguously even across pagan myths. Certainly the notions of resurrection or revival in the myths did not connote the same reality as the gospel meaning of the resurrection. Yet the concept of resurrection was used by some in such a way as to suggest an explicit continuity, without distinction, between Jesus on the one hand and, on the other hand, Tammuz, Adonis, Attis, Dionysus, Osiris, and others. My memories of the discourse of the stranger on the train became very clear: The man had attempted to lead me to question a kind of faith in Jesus that was, in the stranger's mind, quite simple-minded. As I look back over the years, I construe my faith as open and able to accommodate various possibilities. I construe the stranger's position as grounded in a kind of false sophistication that fails to challenge its own assumptions.

My second understanding was that the stranger on the train had a hidden agenda. The hidden agenda of my fellow passenger was similar to the agendas of others with whom I subsequently discussed philosophical and theological issues. They were quick to find fragile, but important, similarities between pagan deities and Jesus of Nazareth to show that Jesus, after all, was "nothing but" a man, and that explanations featuring elements of the supernatural were altogether outdated in the light of "higher criticism." This agenda furthered 18th-19th century Deist and liberal Protestant arguments that Jesus was but a man who experienced apotheosis only in the minds of his immediate followers. It also advanced the secularist propaganda that Jesus was but a human hero in the long line of heroes who extend back to mythological times. There was nothing at all wondrous about his life or death. He was a great teacher, but this stuff about actually rising from the dead was a superstition unworthy of an educated person. All of reality for an "educated" person (I was told by scientific naturalists) must be interpreted and explained without reference to supernatural agencies.

What serves as a philosophical ground for the secularist cause, and for both liberal Protestantism and for liberal Catholics enamored of liberal Protestant hermeneutical assumptions, is a tendency of hostility toward any Christian belief that is not essentially Deist. If I believed that God created a world that existed in time, and a human race that existed in history, and then no longer had anything to do with that world and human race, I would see the development of the natural world and human history as a more or less random series of events that bear no stamp of God's involvement. The remote god of the Deist does not enter into the world, into human events, nor into human interpretive consciousness. Historical happenings have no inner coherence because they are simply the sole consequences, for the Deist, of random and blind circumstances.

To believe that God acts in human history, and to connect this belief with a discernment of historic events (including pagan myths) as ordinated toward some quite marvelous goal is to believe ineluctably in a God who brings intelligibility to all of human existence. To believe in God is to believe that all events are somehow connected because God "entered" into the process of human history when he fashioned human beings and when he redeemed them in the death and resurrection of Jesus. To believe in the Deist god is to believe that human events are not part of a larger story; to believe in the God for whom all things are possible is to believe that human events are the warp and woof of a coherent tapestry that tells a larger tale.

The most important understanding which came from my reading of *The Golden Bough,* an understanding related directly to my understanding of God as One Who Acts in human history, was that the resurrected Jesus fulfilled the always ambiguous prophecies not only of the Old Testament but, more surprisingly, the more cryptic dreams of pagan humanity that arose out of the archetypal structures of the human psyche. I return to this notion in the next chapter.

The foregoing review of dying and rising gods is based largely on Frazer's *The Golden Bough.* Readers are invited to examine other accounts of the gods. Nothing I have read about the so-called resurrections of gods and goddesses is substantively similar to the gospel narratives about Jesus. Nor do various renditions of the pagan myths resemble the content of the living witness of Christian tradition as it refers to the resurrection of Jesus. Among most accounts of the gods there is a great variability. While there is some variability in the gospel accounts of Jesus' resurrection, it is not at all comparable with the variances that occur in mythic accounts of the gods. The apparent discrepancies among the gospel accounts of the resurrection, on the other hand, are indicators of verisimilitude in the testimony of those who experienced the risen Jesus. More about this is forthcoming in chapter five.

Pagan and Christian Rituals

Lex orandi, lex credendi. Very loosely translated this means that a community's religious beliefs follow upon the prayer and worship activities of the community. More broadly it suggests that there is a correspondence, for generally consistent persons, between how they worship and what they believe. The manner in which we pray and worship, to a great extent, delineates the content of our belief. This is true in respect to Christian liturgies and might naturally be assumed to be true regarding pagan cultic activities. There is a great discontinuity, however, between the mystery religions that were prominent in the early centuries of the Christian era and the worship activities of early Christians. Also, there was a decided difference in reference to lifestyle between pagans and early Christians who lived the Christian ideal.

It has already been shown above that pagan mystery religions were based on "once upon a time" myths which were, in turn, the outgrowth of mythic archetypes. The religious beliefs of most pagans, therefore, were inchoate and unformed at best. They were certainly not the kind of religious beliefs most Christians hold today: acts of response to the God of history who speaks in human history. This is not to disparage natural authentic religious values held by sincere pagans, but to indicate a significant difference between Christian beliefs and the belief systems developed by pagans on the basis of their natural experiences. What follows below is a general description of the content of two mystery religions—the mysteries of Dionysus and Mithras. These mystery religions may be taken as representative of the principal religions that competed with early Christianity. These descriptive accounts are followed by some generalizations which differentiate pagan cults from early Christian worship.

The Mysteries of Dionysus

The Greek god Dionysus (the Roman Bacchus, the god of wine) is said to have taken many forms and different faces. The multiple aspects of this god as he is presented in myth are shown also in the multiple forms of religious mysteries that celebrated his divinity. Those who worshiped Dionysus saw his presence in the uncooked flesh of beasts, in the drinking of wine, in the symbol of the phallus, and in the human soul. Those who were confronted with the presence of the god and possessed by him "might feel his power variously: in ecstasy, in inebriation, in sexuality, in spiritual bliss."[2]

According to Marvin Meyer, the mysteries of Dionysus varied from one locale to another and little is known about the actual events that occurred in the mysteries. It is very likely that the mysteries included eating and drinking. The tearing apart of an animal and eating its raw flesh was thought to bestow upon the worshiper the strength and vigor of the beast. Such a practice probably characterized the more archaic form of the mystery. The eating of the flesh of a sacrificed bull, for example, was thought to confer the power of the animal on those who ate the flesh. In some cases, the eating of the testicles of a sacrificed bull—something reserved for prominent members of the cult—was thought to be the most effective remedy against sexual and other dysfunctions. In less savage forms of the mystery, the drinking of wine and various ritual sexual practices were most likely foremost. What was putatively accomplished in these mysteries was not only the attainment of the strength of the god but also a propitiation which turned away the anger of the god.

Depictions of the Dionysian mysteries are several. In Rome the secret initiation into the mysteries included promiscuity accompanied by loud noises produced by clanging cymbals, banging on drums, and loud shriekings. Both women and men were included in the festive rites which included obscenities of every kind. The noise was created allegedly to cover up the screams of the new initiates who were sexually violated in the darkness, something prescribed in the rite. During the ritual, various participants with disheveled hair appeared to be out of their wits as they whirled and turned in frenzied convulsions while they shouted prophecies. Such practices replicated the actions of the whirling dervishes of the eastern Mediterranean. Roman authorities became very concerned about the adverse effects on society that were attributable to the mysteries because the initiates of the mysteries seemed to threaten the moral order of Roman society.

In a more moderate form, the Dionysian mysteries seemed to be little more than activities of a drinking club with religious overtones. Prospective new members were required to lodge a notice of candidature with the club's authorities. Once individuals were approved by the membership, new candidates were required to pay an entrance fee. Members of the Bacchic Society met on the ninth of each month, according to one set of regulations, on the anniversary of the foundation of the Society, and on all feasts of Bacchus or Dionysus. Various fines were prescribed in membership rules. A particularly steep fine was levied on those who got into fights. The priest of the Society performed services during the meetings and members took the roles, by lot, of Kore (Persephone), a simple rustic, Aphrodite, Dionysus, and other gods. The nature of the cultic drama that was enacted is unknown. Meetings were directed by a priest who conducted the sacrifices, a vice-priest, an arch-bacchos, and a treasurer. Members of the society seemed to agree on a central religious rule: Nothing is forbidden. This fits well with the image of the god Dionysus who was celebrated as the "loud-roaring and reveling" god who was also savage, warlike, ineffable, bull-faced, howling, and pure. This last characteristic of the god, purity, points out the multi-faceted nature of the god. Dionysus contained even contradictions within himself.

Mystery religions, by definition, are concerned with arcane beliefs and secret rituals. We know little about the inner dynamics of mystery religions because we know so little about the specific practices entailed in these religions. Nonetheless, it seems that devotees of Dionysus struggled to attain identification with the god through participation in practices that today may seem outlandish and even immoral. The goal of eternal life through identification with the god is certainly an understandable religious goal. The means by which this goal was approached, however, grew out of moral distortions and fables created in archaic and sometime savage societies.

The Mysteries of Mithras

Mithraism was the worship of Mithras, the Indo-Iranian god of Light. Mithras was the chief ally of the Ahura Mazda, the principal force of good in the ancient Zoroastrian religion. The worship of Mithras attained popularity in the Roman world around the time of the emergence of Christianity on the world scene and challenged Christianity for the hearts of men who were seeking a religious basis in their lives. It is often said that Mithras was the last pagan god dethroned by Christianity. Women were explicitly excluded from this mystery religion.

Mithraism eventually fell to Christianity in the struggle for the commitment of the peoples of the Mediterranean world under the sway of Rome. Mithraism, in fact, resembled Christianity to some extent in the solemnity of its ritual, a moral code that challenged devotees to courage and loyalty, and the promise of immortality it offered. When Christianity eventually won out, it assimilated some of the incidentals of Mithraism, particularly some of the things Christians today associate with Christmas.

Mithras was associated with Sol, the Sun god. In some instances the names Mithras and Sol were applied in such a way as to suggest an identification of both gods. Mithras is known in Persian mythology as the god who pilfered a bull and then slew it with a dagger. The blood of the bull spilled upon the ground and from it grew herbs, health-giving plants, wheat, and the vine. The sacrifice of the mythic bull is said to have occurred in a cave. Mithraism was brought to the city of Rome by soldiers who became familiar with the religion in the eastern outposts of the empire. As the god of light and truth, the festival of Mithras was celebrated in Rome during the winter solstice. The sun appears to be born each year on December 25th. It is then that the sun's reign begins again after months of challenge by the darkness; the forces of light overcome the forces of darkness. The festival of *Sol Invictus,* the Unconquered Sun, was appropriated by the Christian Church by the end of the third century in the West and as late as 375 A.D. in the East as the day on which the nativity of Jesus would be celebrated. Christians were instructed not to worship the sun as did the heathens but to adore the Creator of the sun. This followed the general practice in early Christianity of assimilating to itself whatever was good or neutral in paganism, and useful for the propagation of the Christian faith. While Christianity was the great annihilator of the evils present in paganism, Christianity was also the great assimilator of anything that was authentically good and human in pagan religions.

The ritual of Mithraism were performed in a cave and included liturgical washings or purifications, ceremonies of initiation, and sacred meals in which the flesh of a bull was eaten along with bread and water mixed with wine. Participation in the sacred banquet was ordered toward salvation and eternal life as well as to the propitiation of the god which procured divine protection. Mircea Eliade indicates that the mythic Mithras was the only god who did not himself undergo the tragic destinies of other gods, i.e., Mithras did not undergo death and experience a resurrection. Prior to their initiation into the mysteries, participants took an oath (*sacramentum*) to keep the mysteries secret. Accompanied by various ceremonies, the initiates of the mysteries advanced in respect to seven classes of participation. The grades of Crow, Bride, Soldier, Lion, Persian, Courier of the Sun, and Father constituted the religious status of devotees of Mithras. Among these grades there were two additional ranks: the servitors and participants; participants were members who had reached the grade of Lion or higher.

Candidates who wished to advance in the religious mystery were required to undergo various ordeals. For example, a candidate was blindfolded with his hands tied behind his back with the intestines of a chicken. He was led to a place where others imitated the cawing of crows and the roaring of lions. The blindfold was removed and the candidate was obliged to jump over a ditch filled with water. Someone would then come with a sword, announced himself as a liberator, and cut the intestines that bound the hands of the candidate. Members of the mystery religion advanced to higher grades in a ritual that simulated murder.

Eliade goes on to observe that Mithraism was disseminated broadly in the ancient world from Scotland in the west to Mesopotamia in the east, from North Africa and Spain to Central Europe and the Balkans. Since the religion was exclusively a cult for soldiers, the mysteries of Mithras spread wherever there was a presence of the Roman legions. For this very reason, contrary to some claims that Mithraism almost won the competition against Christianity, it is unlikely Mithraism could ever have become a serious threat to Christianity.[4]

Christianity and Mystery Religions

It has been surmised generally that Christianity was based not only on the Jewish religion and the Hebrew Testament, but also took some of its forms and early practices from the Greco-Roman world in which it was spread. Many early Christian practices, for some critics, are little more than extensions of pagan religious practices. These same critics would have it that Christianity was simply a natural outgrowth of pagan myths and cultic activities. That is, Christianity is viewed as one mystery religion among many others with which Christianity shared symbols, beliefs, and worship activities. It is not difficult, however, to demonstrate a substantial difference between Christianity and pagan mystery religions.

Paganism and Christianity: Differences

The historian Robin Lane Fox, by some accounts a non-believer himself, states that almost all of the continuities cited between pagan religious practices and Christianity are spurious. He notes, for example, that the Christian teaching of charity and the worth of the poor, along with the introduction of the idea of sin, constituted something new within the Roman empire at large.[5]

What Fox uncovered in his research pertaining to pagan cults supports his claim of a marginal and weak connection between paganism and Christianity. First, pagan rites were not explicitly connected with any particular religious creed or doctrine. These cultic acts frequently involved animal sacrifices which were gifts to the gods, but cannot be construed as expressions of coherent beliefs. Pagan myths and cults generally evolved separately, and were conjoined incidentally at a later time. While the principle *Lex orandi, lex credendi* is applicable to Christianity, the principle does not necessarily and strictly apply to pagan cults since no intrinsic relationship existed as a matter of course between cultic acts and the myths that were later joined to cultic activities. What is certain, however, is this: there was at least an *implicit* connection between what pagan cultists believed and what they practiced in their rituals.

Nor were pagans exhorted to respond to divinely revealed truths. They were not counseled to develop any kind of religious faith in the gods in the sense Christians were exhorted to accept God's will and his divine truths trustfully. The notion of heresy as used later by Christians to preserve the Christian tradition was not used in the same sense as pagans. For the pagans, heresy did not mean a false doctrine but instead a different school of philosophical thought. Fox observes that the difference between pagan cult acts and Christian worship acts is obvious in the very way Christians were tested as enemies of the empire. Pagans could not understand why Christians would not pay a gesture of worship to a pagan god since such a gesture, for the pagans, did not imply anything about one's formal religious beliefs. In the Roman empire, for example, a cultic act performed in honor of a god was not construed as a repudiation of the Christian's one true God. The concept of the one true God in the Roman mind did not exist. Monotheism could not be comprehended by the polytheistic mind.[6]

"Any account of pagan worship which minimizes the god's uncertain anger and mortal's fear of it is an empty account," according to Fox.[7] In their cultic acts pagans were primarily concerned with the propitiation of the gods. Favors were sought from the gods and any thanks given to the gods was connected to sentiments of propitiation and fear of the gods' anger. Remember, when we think of pagan gods we must think of deities whose moods changed with each passing wind. Today a god might be favorable toward a person for no particular reason; tomorrow the god might be unfavorable on no particular account. These gods needed to be soothed regularly.

Pagans and Christians: Further Discontinuities

Another historian of pagan mystery religions, Walter Burkert, states that the mystery religions of late antiquity—so interesting because they surround the emergence of Christianity in human history—were not at all religions in the contemporary use of the word. Generally, pagan mystery religions appeared simply as options within a conglomerate of ancient religions. Ancient mystery religions were initiations that brought about a personal change of status in relation to a god or goddess. This change, however, was removed from any visible change of outward status. Initiation was a voluntary personal choice that aimed a change of mind of the initiate through a structured experience of the sacred. Faith of a sort was required in order to gain a vague salvation. "It is tempting to assume the central idea of all initiations should be death and resurrection...but the pagan evidence for resurrection symbolism is uncompelling at best."[8] One would suspect, notes Burkert, that the cult supposed by some to have mounted a challenge to Christianity—Mithraism—would have emphasized resurrection since the idea of immortality and the ascent of the righteous to heaven was well established in Iranian Zoroastrianism from which Mithraism emerged. The evidence for such a supposition is lacking.

The imagery of Mithraism was on the same level as the speculations of philosophers regarding the afterlife. There was no special content of faith nor foundation for faith; there was no redirection of religious belief toward other-worldly concerns. Burkert observes that a pagan initiate of a mystery cult would have judged Christians, on the evidence of their burial places, members of a religion excessively concerned with death and decay. Mystery religions resembled votive religions through which initiates largely sought protection from dangers, cures of illnesses, and a generalized kind of blessedness. "Mysteries, like votive religion, remained to some extent, an experimental form of religion."[9]

Burkert also points out the differences among pagan mystery cults in respect to social organization and coherence. None of the cult models approach the Christian model of a church. Mystery cults were organized along three forms. Some cults were originated by itinerant clergy or wandering priests who initiated others into the secrets of the cult. In this form the wandering seer or priest made a craft out of the sacred, a craft that was usually passed from father to son for generations. In another form clergy or priests were to be found at a particular sanctuary. Some of these sanctuaries, particularly in the Greek world, were administered by the leaders of the *polis* or town. In the near East and Egypt the sanctuaries were often self sustaining. A great deal of wealth could be accumulated by the priests in time of war or from gifts dedicated to the god or goddess of the shrine.

Finally, the third type of organization was the common association or "club" or sodality. Individuals remained independent but they contributed to the general coming together of equals in common religious interest, e.g., initiations, sacrifices, and ceremonial meals. Of all of these, the organization that was to win most favor was the local sanctuary with a permanently stationed clergy. None of these forms of organization came close to the Christian model of church. In Christianity there were articles of faith to be confessed while in descriptions of mystery cults there is usually a reference to the stages of initiations that took place. Pagan gods, in the context of mystery religions, are never seriously jealous of one another. As we have seen above, there was no concept of heresy as we know it today. Persons could become initiates of various competing cults. Lines of distinction between one cult and another—in terms of the profession of a constant faith on the part of the initiates—were absent.

There was no sense, in the pagan cults, of members' obligations to a definite moral code that was to be followed in the adoration of a god or goddess. Christians, on the other hand, refused integration into the larger society when such an integration was symbolized by sacrifices to the gods. Christians rejected any assimilation into the regnant pagan culture and any irenic attempt to dilute the Christian message by merging this message with pagan myth. Christians were bound to rear their children in the fear of the Lord. The Christian faith was to be handed down to new generations, something that would have seemed strange to members of pagan cults. With a new morality "ousting all the well-established forms of population control such as the exposure of children, homosexuality, and prostitution, the *ekklesia* became a self-reproducing type of community that could not be stopped."[10] The social organization and coherence of the Christian church, vastly different from the social organization and norms for coherence in pagan cults, was a large factor in the survival of Christianity. Christians believe, of course, that this factor was not merely accidental but that it discloses, at least in some small way, the protective hand of God in human history.

Concluding Remarks

Upon close examination and careful analysis, the resurrection of Jesus and the so-called resurrection of pagan deities have little in common. Those who promote the idea that Jesus was but one more hero in a long train of heroes, and that the risen Jesus is on the same level as, say, Adonis or Attis, cannot formulate effective arguments for this claim on the basis of valid evidence. Further, the early Christian church was not a mere outgrowth of pagan mystery cults; the entire notion of church as known by early Christian was foreign to the consciousness of pagans.

Strip away the surface of claims that the resurrection of Jesus is "nothing but" another myth of a dying and reviving god and one will find a philosophical orientation toward reality that was born in the

Enlightenment period of intellectual history. The attempt to confuse the resurrection of Jesus, moreover, with the so-called resurrections of pagan gods has been more a projection of Enlightenment hostility toward Christianity[11]—under the cover of "higher criticism" and "scientific hermeneutic methods"[12]—than the result of careful study and critical scholarship. Also to be found are interpretive assumptions that are not as defensible as they seem at a first superficial glance.

This is not to say there are no similarities between paganism and Christianity, between accounts of revived gods and the resurrected Jesus. There are similarities. All human beings experience the resurrection motif in nature and in their lives. These experiences give rise to a resurrection archetype or profound meaning structure in the human psyche. It is from this archetype, as is shown in the following chapter, that pagan resurrection myths are projected; it is this archetype that inclines the human imagination to view the resurrection of Jesus as something possible and even appropriate.

Notes to Chapter 2

1. The full narratives about these gods can be found in James Frazer's *The New Golden Bough,* ed. Theodor H. Gaster (New York: S. G. Phillips, Inc. 1972), 283–397.
2. Marvin W. Meyer, *The Ancient Mysteries: A Sourcebook* (San Francisco: Harper & Row, 1987), 64. A number of ancient sources relevant to the Dionysian mysteries—including Euripides, Plato, and Livy—are included in Meyer's book. See 67–109.
3. Ibid., 105.
4. Mircea Eliade, *A History of Religious Ideas: From Gautama Buddha to the Triumph of Christianity,* trans. Willard Trask (Chicago: The University of Chicago Press, 1984), 324–326.
5. Robin Lane Fox, *Pagans and Christians* (New York: Alfred A. Knopf, Inc., 1987), 22.
6. Ibid., 31.
7. Ibid., 38.
8. Walter Burkert, *Ancient Mystery Cults* (Cambridge, MA: Harvard University Press, 1987), 27.
9 . Ibid., 28–29.

3

...SURRECTION ARCHETYPE

This ch[...]d of four parts. First, pagan resurrection myths a[...]nditions that forestructured the minds and hearts of ancie[...]ception of the message of the risen Jesus. These myths, fa[...]lated to God's providential workings in human history, co[...]ration for the heralding of the good news of Jesus' resurrectio[...]vangelization of sorts. Pagan myths, in other words, play an impo[...]nt part, subsidiary to the part played by Judaism and the prophets, in the economy of divine revelation.

Second, the concept of myth as a mode of truth is investigated. It is necessary for us to understand pagan myths in a new way. While the message of the resurrection of Jesus is discontinuous in major aspects with pagan resurrection myths, there are undeniable thematic continuities between the message of the resurrection of Jesus and various pagan myths of renewal. There is some sense in which the message of Jesus' resurrection and pagan myths are comparable; both the resurrection of Jesus and pagan myths of revival point to the renovation of all creation by God. The message embedded in nature and the message signified in Jesus' resurrection is the same: The cosmos is in process of being created. In its end will it find its beginning.

Third, God is named as the God of the archetypes; these archetypes are somehow situated in the collective unconscious of the race. A conceptual framework is borrowed from the work of the depth psychology of Carl Gustav Jung to show how God is the author of psychic archetypes. The archetypes in the collective unconscious were developed over thousands of years on the basis of the common experiences of humankind. God is the author of the external world in which human experience occurs and the author of the psychological mechanisms by which human experiences are registered. God is, therefore, the author of those primal meaning structures we call archetypes.

Fourth, the thematic continuities between the message of the risen Jesus and pagan resurrection myths are considered in respect to what Jung called the resurrection archetype. I borrow his nomenclature but redefine the concept of resurrection archetype. The resurrection archetype is a profoundly human meaning structure, a paradigm that is "hard-wired" in the initial structure of the psyche and developed by means of universal human experience. The origin and source of the resurrection archetype is also explicated in reference to common human experiences that center on what I label the death and resurrection theme. This theme or motif is manifested widely and dramatically in the natural world. The resurrection archetype, I believe, is an *a priori* element of being human in that the capacity to learn from human experience gives origin to the resurrection archetype. This element is augmented by experiences of the death and resurrection theme during the course of the human lifespan.

The chapter concludes with a brief examination of the work of the resurrection archetype in making the resurrection of Jesus an event that is credible and worthy of belief. Millions of Christians find the message of Jesus' resurrection credible and even suasive because, in part, the message resonates with the resurrection archetype in the human collective unconscious. The resurrection archetype or meaning structure is an internal witness of the plausibility of the resurrection of Jesus.

Pagan Myth and Christian Message

It must be admitted that not all early Christians may have understood the message of Jesus' resurrection precisely. Some early Christians may have grasped the notion of Jesus' resurrection as a marvelous new myth. How else explain Paul's admonition to the Corinthians concerning the resurrection? "If Christ has not been raised, your faith is futile and you are still in your sins. Then those who have died in Christ have perished. If for this life only we have hoped in Christ, we are of all people most to be pitied. But in fact Christ has been raised from the dead, the first fruits of those who have died" (1 Cor 15: 17-20). It would not have been unusual for some who had been brought up to believe in myths to imagine initially that the message of Jesus' resurrection was of the same class as pagan myths of rebirth and renewal.

Nor is it unlikely that early Christians who fully accepted the bodily resurrection of Jesus, particularly non-Jews in the Greco-Roman world, were untouched prior to their conversion by mythic recitals and rituals associated with themes of renewal. It is likely that the good news of the risen Jesus found eager reception in those whose psyches had been forestructured by familiar pagan myths, including so-called pagan resurrection myths.

Just as there are many psychological types of believers today within the Christian tradition and many believers who are at various stages of faith development, there were probably different types of believers in the first century of our era. One type of believer, perhaps, found a haven—at least in the initial stage of faith development—in a Christian community simply because the Christian experience met the needs of individuals for community activity and religious worship. It would not have been difficult for this type of early Christian believer to accept the good news—again, initially but not necessarily permanently—on the basis of a prior familiarity with a pagan ritual of renewal and membership in some sort of worshiping community that represented a kind of "experimental" religion.

It is probable, then, that some Christians failed to differentiate adequately between the good news of the risen Jesus and the rebirth of fabulous characters among the *dramatis personae* of pagan mythology. Christians who moved beyond the initial stages of faith development in terms of understanding the good news, however, ordinarily distinguished between the heralding of the risen Jesus and the narration of "once upon a time" stories of pagan mythology.

Pagan Resurrection Myths and Providence

To say that some early Christians responded favorably to the heralding of the risen Jesus because their minds and imaginations were forestructured previously by exposure to pagan myths of rebirth and renewal is to raise the important issue of divine providence. Providentially, it is maintained, just as Roman roads were appropriated by Christian missionaries and the Greek language used for the spreading of the Christian message throughout the Mediterranean world, so also was human consciousness made ready by pagan resurrection myths for the message of the risen Jesus. Of course, those Deists who believe that God simply created the world and thereafter left it to its own devices explicitly deny the notion of divine providence. For those who affirm human history as revelatory, for those who affirm that God speaks in human history and in the natural world, the concept of divine providence follows ineluctably. [1]

To believe in the God of the Hebrew Bible and the New Testament is to believe in a God who is close to his people, a God who cares for his people as the sheep of his flock and provides for them according to their needs. The god who created the world and sent it on its way without any ongoing providential interaction with the world (the god of Deism) is a god who, for all practical purposes, might as well not exist. Deism is one step removed from atheism. To believe in a god who is irrelevant to human history is to believe in no God at all. To believe in God is to affirm God's revelatory and providential presence in nature and in history.

The notion of divine providence, of course, can be understood very simplistically and caution must be used to prevent falling into naive conceptions of providence. Providence is not a script for human beings written out in advance by God. Providence does not annul human freedom but instead works to help human beings exercise their freedom in the choice of the various options set before them. Nor is divine providence a rigid plan for the process of human history. Providence always works in history within the context of human freedom. Providence is not predestination. It is not without difficulty that any particular event in human history can be categorized as providential. Historical events often must be viewed in long retrospect before their providential significance can be supposed.

The basic meaning of divine providence, however, is clear: God is not remote from what he created. God is involved in human history and discloses himself in particular events. God "speaks" within the process of human history to guide this process toward some kind of ultimate fulfillment and to prepare human beings for this ultimate fulfillment of history and creation itself. He also prepares human beings for continued dialogue with himself and for the ongoing revelatory process. Not to believe in a God who is provident, one who acts in human history in mysterious ways, is the equivalent of not believing in the God of the Judaeo-Christian tradition.

It is claimed here that through the workings of divine providence various pagan resurrection myths inclined the hearts and minds of individuals toward the eventual heralding of the good news of the risen Jesus. Without the experience of pagan resurrection myths, many individuals at the beginning of the Christian era might not have been equipped psychically and spiritually for the reception of good news of Jesus' bodily resurrection. This claim requires that we begin to look at pagan myth in a new way. Indeed, it suggests strongly that the God of history utilized even pagan resurrection myths in some manner in the service of the risen Jesus. If the faith of some early Christians in the risen Jesus was made possible because their minds

and imaginations were forestructured by their encounters with pagan resurrection myths, is this not to imply that some truth and goodness were to
be found in pagan myths?

Truth and Myth

We are prone today to think of pagan myths as outrageous stories having
no foundation in the real world. These stories often contain contradictory
points of view and sometimes include gross or lewd story lines. We know
that what is found in mythic stories never happened within the bounds of
actual human history. Despite this many honorable and intelligent individuals in pre-Christian times somehow embraced myths as symbols of religious
commitment, symbols in the sense of rudimentary creedal formulations.
This occurred because many informed and educated pagans—individuals
with at least as much common sense as ourselves—found something of
truth in their myths.

In an astute treatise on the nature of myth, *Did the Greeks Believe in Their
Myths?*, Paul Veyne argues that myth is truthful but only figuratively so. "It
is not historical truth mixed with lies; it is a high philosophical teaching
that is entirely true, on the condition that instead of taking it literally, one
sees in it an allegory." [2] Pagan myths were not taken at their face value by
those who knew how to encounter them. They were taken as allegorical
expositions of various truths, expositions that required interpretation. In
order to speak truthfully about mythic stories it was first necessary to determine what profound truths were clothed in the allegorical vestments of
the myth. At its surface a myth was often nothing more than a fanciful story.
Once interpreted by someone with insight into the grammar of allegory, the
truths hidden in the myth were disclosed. The myth of Athena being born
from the head of Zeus, notes Veyne in reference to the interpretation of
Chrysippus, contains the truth that technical knowledge is communicated
by speech, "which is centered in the head." [3]

Not every thinker of antiquity taught that the interpretation of myths
led to authentic knowledge. Enough of these thinkers, however, constructed
powerful arguments to show that truth often dwells within myths and even
reveals something of the meaning structures that exist within human minds
and hearts. I return to this point later in the chapter. Nor do all contemporary scholars of the philosophy of mythology agree that myth constitutes an
analogical or allegorical explanation of something. Lawrence Hatab argues

for a pluralistic conception of truth. This conception would permit different forms of understanding and different forms of truth. Rational, scientific, and philosophical forms of understanding, Hatab avers, have wrongly displaced the truth that is myth.[4] Science, we suppose, has explained myth in a systematic way when all that science has done is reduce myth to so-called scientific categories. To say this in another way, science has reduced classical myth to the categories of scientific mythology.

To define myth in terms of anthropology, comparative religion, psychology, sociology, or any empirical science or philosophy, according to Hatab, is to have missed the point of the meaning of myth. "A myth is not *meant* to be an explanation but rather a presentation of something which can *not* be explained (in the sense of an objective account)." [5] In another place Hatab states that myth is not an explanation but a "*presentation* of the arrival/withdrawal of existential meaning." [6]

A myth stands forth as an unveiling in the original sense of the Greek word *aletheia* (truth): a myth is an uncovering of some profound mystery, an unconcealment in itself that does not require further rational explanation. Originally, I suggest, myth stood forth not as discursive writing (for discursive writing implies systematic and step-by-step rationality), but as the oral announcement and/or ritual enactment of a profound mystery in the lives of the community members who were within earshot of the announcement. The narrating of a myth of the hunt in archaic times in tribal societies, for example, disclosed something to members of the tribal community sitting around the campfire about the mysteries and sacred dimensions of the world. The game that was hunted and caught was provided out of the largesse of the world and the world's Maker. The response to the standing forth of such a myth is thankfulness on the part of those who would share in the feast. Any other response would be taken in archaic times to fall short of what was appropriate. The truly human response to the recital of a myth is not analytic and logical but instead a prelogical sense of awe at the sacred mystery offered by the myth.

A proper myth, I would argue, may be both a presentation of a mystery and also a non-discursive explanation (in the sense of a ritual elaboration of a mystery). Further, it is probable the meaning of myth itself underwent development over time and came to take on various senses. Myths, for those who attend to them respectfully, provide valuable insights into various ways of thinking about the world and insights about the human presence in the world. A myth may also present a sacred mystery and at the same time serve to explain some aspect of the lives of those who respond positively to the myth.

This is the not the place to reconcile the possible different meanings of myth. Such a reconciliation would go beyond the scope of this book. Suffice it to observe that there are perhaps several senses in which myth can be viewed as a form of truth. A myth is conceived and gestated in the profound depths of the human psyche. Once expressed, a myth can be a form of truth about the world at large, about the human condition, and/or about the individuals in whom the myth finds resonance.

As noted previously, there are great discontinuites between the resurrection of Jesus and pagan resurrection myths. There are also continuities, however, The resurrection of Jesus unconceals a cosmic truth decisively, a truth that was only insinuated in the universal human experiences of the resurrection motif in nature. These experiences were varied, multiple, and impactful. The experience of waking up each morning, for example, can easily be viewed as a resurrection analogue. More than this, pagan resurrection myths promised faintly and confusedly what the resurrection of Jesus promised decisively: the world is in the process of redemptive creation; the world and everything in it will emerge from death into glory. The author of Romans said it best: "We know that the whole creation has been groaning in labor pains until now; and not only the creation, but we ourselves, who have the first fruits of the Spirit, groan inwardly while we wait for adoption, the redemption of our bodies" (Romans 8:22,23).

God of the Archetypes

Some of the thematic similarities between the Christian message and pagan myths led prospective converts in the early Church to raise questions that called into question the uniqueness of Jesus. "Were the stories about Jesus nothing but myths on par with myths about other fabulous beings?" The early apologist Justin Martyr (a philosopher who converted to Christianity early in the second century of our era) recognized this apologetic problem. For example, Justin wrote in his *First Apology* that "Aesculapius, who, though he was a great physician, was struck by a thunderbolt, and so ascended to heaven; and Bacchus, too, after he had been torn limb from limb; and Hercules, when he had committed himself to the flames to escape his toils...and Perseus the son of Danae; and Bellerophon, who, though sprung from mortals, rose to heaven on the horse Pegasus." [7] There were, indeed, some thematic similarities between the message of Jesus' resurrection and ascension on the one hand and the myths that dealt with the deaths of pagan heroes and their rising to heaven.

Justin's argument, by which he showed the uniqueness of Jesus' death and resurrection, centered on the role of the evil demons or fallen angels. Familiar with the prophecies about the Messiah in the Hebrew Testament, the wicked demons fabricated myths to spread confusion and "to deceive and lead astray the human race. For having heard it proclaimed through the prophets that the Christ was to come, and that the ungodly among men were to be punished by fire, they put forward many to be called sons of Jupiter, under the impression that they would be able to produce in men the idea that the things which were said with regard to Christ were mere marvelous tales, like the things which were said by the poets." [8]

Justin's argument perhaps has some merit today among many Christians. His explanation was simple and direct. The argument, however, has always seemed a bit labored to me. For me the wicked demons always resembled convenient devices pulled out of a hat to explain away difficulties. It seems there is a much better argument to account for the thematic similarities between the resurrection of Jesus and pagan myths of renewal. This argument or explanation focuses on what I call the resurrection archetype.

What is an Archetype?

The notion of archetype is perhaps associated more often with the psychological theories of Carl Gustav Jung (1875-1961) than with any other scholar or writer. The notion of archetype cannot be understood except in relation to Jung's concept of the unconscious. The unconscious is the "receptable of all lost memories and of all contents that are still too weak to be conscious." [9] These contents of the unconscious are also products of what Jung called associative activity. It is such activity in which dreams arise. In addition to these components there are repressions of painful thoughts and feelings. The sum of all these contents is called the "personal unconscious." Also, there are, in a deeper area of the psyche, elements not individually acquired but inherited by virtue of one's membership in the human race. There are "*a priori* inborn forms of 'intuition,' namely, the *archetypes* of perception and apprehension, which are the *a priori* determinants of all psychic processes." [10] Jung goes on to note that just as human instincts make us tend to a specifically human mode of existence, so also do archetypal ways of perception and apprehension guide us into actions which are particularly human. According to Jung, human instincts and archetypal patterns constitute the "collective unconscious" of the race.

"There are present in every individual," wrote Jung, "besides his personal memories, the great 'primordial' images...the inherited possibilities of human

.imagination as it was from time immemorial. The fact of this inheritance explains the truly amazing phenomenon that certain motifs from myths and legends repeat themselves the world over in identical forms." [11]

Among the most notable archetypes is the archetype of rebirth. Jung notes five different aspects of rebirth: Metempsychosis, reincarnation, rebirth within the span of an individual life, resurrection, and transformation. The latter two aspects of this archetype are pertinent here. Resurrection means the reestablishment of life after death. At its highest level of interpretation "it is assumed that the resurrection of dead is the raising up of the *corpus glorificationis*, the 'subtle body', in a state of incorruptibility."[12] Transformation is understand not as passing through death to life directly but instead by participation in a ritual. While rebirth may be understood in several senses, the fact that it archetypally refers both to something akin to the resurrection of Christ and the Christian sacrament of baptism (through which individuals are born into the death and resurrection of Christ) is salient.

At this point I must indicate that Jung himself, it seems, did not believe in God in any ordinary sense. He did express belief in "differentiated expressions or aspects of one ineffable truth." Of the resurrection of Jesus, Jung wrote: "I know of resurrection only because it is a very important archetypal idea. I don't know whether it has ever occurred as a physical fact. I see no point in believing in something I don't know." [13] At best, perhaps, Jung was an agnostic, a child of 19th century scientism. Some of his ideas, however, can be re-interpreted in an attempt to gain further insight into the resurrection of Jesus.

Archetypes, in my way of thinking, are universal meaning structures of the human psyche. These meaning structures comprise the psychic infrastructure which supports the genesis of certain widespread ideas, symbols, and myths. I suggest that archetypes are the foundations of the sense we have when we sometimes use the word heart. "I know in my heart," we say, "that Christ is risen." The knowledge we grasp in our hearts is meta-rational or extra-rational but not irrational; it is often unexplainable in terms of logic. "The heart has its reasons," wrote Blaise Pascal, "of which reason knows nothing...it is the heart which perceives God and not the reason. That is what faith is: God perceived by the heart, not by the reason." [14] Cardinal Newman maintained that we receive the Word of God in faith on two grounds. First, we trust the messenger. Second, we discern the message as likely. We have a keen sense of the intrinsic excellence of the message; the message is such that it is grasped as something from God. The source of this keen sense, it could be said, is archetypal. Those who are of God, Newman seems to say, will hear God's message. Someone responds positively to the message of the resurrection of Jesus does so because at the core of that person's being there is an obediential potency. [15]

Archetypes are universal. This universality is due in part to the human nature that all human beings share and also to the common experiences of all human beings. The intuitions, idea, and images that proceed from the archetypes in the form of myths and rituals are also universal.

The influence of archetypes on human beliefs and behavior is exemplified in the archetype of birth, growth, and rebirth represented in a symbolic sense by the image of water. In the common experience of humankind, water has been viewed as central to life in many ways. Grains, fruits, and vegetables do not grow without rain water or irrigation. The birth of babies is usually introduced by the flow of the amniotic waters or "water of life." It is impossible to exist without the refreshing water that brings surcease of thirst. Water is used also as a cleansing agent. In times of floods water is capable of destroying everything in its path. It is no wonder, then, that the presence of water has played a large role in myths of creation. If water is so important in daily life, it must have been present at the beginning of the world. This intuition, arising from archetypal meaning structures, prompted many mythmakers the world over to locate the genesis of the world in the midst of water. The significance of water moved others, quite naturally, to develop rituals of cleansing and rebirth that featured the use of water. The universal symbol of water, used in Christian baptism, was the most meaningful symbol possible to dramatize rebirth and/or cleansing from sin. In a certain sense the symbol of water as a baptismal symbol—a symbol that arose naturally out of the depths of the human psyche—was created as a sacramental symbol by the Creator at the very beginning. Water, associated with life, growth, and renewal in the natural world, became a symbol for supernatural life, growth, and renewal.

What is apparent in any investigation of the archetype of birth, growth, and renewal is that this archetype came into being because of the universal experiences of humankind, experiences that were often associated with water. This archetype or psychic meaning structure originated on the basis of common human experiences. The profound meaning structures within ourselves came into existence because the world was made according to a particular divine plan and not according to some other plan. The structure of the natural world as experienced by humanity demarcated the meaning structures of the human psyche. *The world is such as it is because of the creative activity of God. The human psyche along with its archetypes is such as it is due to God's creative agency. God is, then, creator of primal meaning structures. God is the God of the archetypes.*

If God is the God of genuine human archetypes because he created both the external world of our experience and the psychic mechanisms by which we experience the world, then God can be said to disclose truth and meaning, to some incalculable extent, in myth. Pagan myths of renewal ordinarily contain mixtures of error along with aspects of truth. What issues from archetypes are ideas and images that are most relevant to the human condition. These ideas and images, however, are often inchoate and nebulous. Further, the ideas and images that originate in the psyche due to the archetypes are filtered through the subjectivities and biases of mythmakers when the archetypal images are expressed consciously. These expressions of primal images occurred during the course of the thousands of years it took for popular myths to develop thereby adding accretions to what was already clouded. Nonetheless many myths contain kernels of truth. Many myths are confused versions of the truth. The seeds of truth and meaning can be found in what myths express, foreshadow, and portend. This is elegantly clear in the case of the resurrection archetype.

The Resurrection Archetype

How to explain the pagan myths of "dying and reviving gods?" What occasioned the myths of Attis, Adonis, Hyacinth, and Osiris? Joseph Campbell has written of the archetype of the collective unconscious and of the great monomyth that has taken shape according to a universal formula. A hero ventures forth from the everyday world and encounters powerful forces. The hero wins a momentous victory and returns from a mysterious adventure to bestow blessings upon the human race. [16] Campbell goes on to discuss several heroes and gods whose stories fit the universal hero paradigm. He includes a reference to Christ in this discussion. Carl Gustav Jung is favorably cited by Campbell as the one who was most insightful and illuminating concerning universal mythic motifs when he, Jung, developed the notion of archetypes of the collective unconscious. "Myths and dreams...are motivated from a single psychophysiological source—namely, the human imagination moved by the conflicting urgencies of the organs (including the brain) of the human body..." [17]

I associate the resurrection archetype with the universal paradigmatic myth of Campbell's hero, the one who overcomes at great personal cost a lurking demon who represents some kind of evil. After the victory, the hero is celebrated as a savior of his people.

This is my thesis: 1) that millennia of human experience and development led to the genesis of a resurrection archetype in the collective unconscious of the race, and 2) that tribal or local heroes became vested in images assigned by the primal archetype that represented hope and victory over death: the resurrection archetype. To long-departed but celebrated tribal heroes, I suspect, were ascribed the archetypal images associated with nature's seasonal triumphs over the death and decay of vegetation. The forces that brought forth these triumphs—forces that were mysterious and divine and absolutely necessary for continued survival—were personified and attributed to the hero already revered by the tribe or locality. In his 1922 summary of the eleven volume set of *The Golden Bough*, Sir James Frazer observed that Osiris, Tammuz, Adonis, and Attis represented the annual decay and revival of life. "In name and detail the rites varied from place to place: in substance they were the same. The supposed death and resurrection of this oriental deity (was) a god of many names but of essentially one nature..." [18] The genealogy of dying and resurrected gods is not difficult to trace, at least at the molar level of theoretical reflection. The images of these gods arise out of the resurrection archetype and are attached by various peoples to their heroes who may have actually existed in the forgotten past.

Origin of the Resurrection Archetype

Out of what human experiences common to humankind did the resurrection archetype originate? The question is eminently important. What shared experiences of humankind over great lengths of time were so profound that an anticipation and even expectation of the overcoming of death became ingrained in the unconscious psychic life of human beings? Why did archetypal ideas and images center on hope against the threat of death, trust in a world that was often tremendously discouraging, and a conviction that there was something further beyond the dissolution of all living things? The image of "rising again" out of a catastrophic termination of life may well have been innate and encompassed in human nature from the beginning of the race. Even if this primal meaning structure was not a given at the beginning of human life on earth, however, this archetype was certainly forged at the anvil of shared human experiences over thousands of years. The collective unconscious of the race developed out of untold human encounters with the repeating cycles of death and resurrection, loss and gain, despair and hope, decay and renewal, dissolution and rebirth, disappearance and appearance, impoverishment and prosperity, and defeat and resurgence that were integral to human existence. The myth of the Phoenix rising from its own ashes to new life could very well be the emblem of humanity even prior to the heralding of the Christian message. All of creation seemed to whisper, perhaps ambiguously, a reason for hope in an ultimate victory over death and dissolution.

1. *Cycles of Vegetation.* We have already seen above that the patterns of agricultural "death" and "rebirth" were experienced each year with much interest on the part of those who would live or die as a result of the harvest. There was a time in human history when Paleolithic hunters focused attention on sacred totems and their mystical relationships with the animals they hunted. Eventually the focus of attention became fixed on agriculture. Religious relations with animals that prevailed in the hunter-gatherer phase of cultural development were displaced by a mystical bond with vegetation according to Mircea Eliade. [19] The place of women in tribal society was enhanced because the child-bearing fruitfulness of the women who tended the fields was associated in tribal myths with the fecundity of the crops. A vastly important contribution to the advancement of civilization was provided by the women who not only tended the fields but also began to develop simple agricultural technologies. The advance of civilization pivoted on the agricultural fortunes of the tribes and villages. If the harvest in a particular place was good, there was cause for great celebration that the gods had listened to the petitions of the people; if the harvest was wanting, there was reason for great sadness since a future possibility was starvation.

All of the concern for the success of the harvest was suffused with a powerful sense of wonder and mystery. Remember that scientific explanations of agricultural processes were unknown. All that was known was that the planting—the burial—of seeds in the early spring conduced later in the year to a harvest that was great or small. If the gods took care to "resurrect" mere buried seeds, might they not also be solicitous for the buried dead? Was not the renewal of flowers, grasses, grains, fruits, and vegetables each year a harbinger of a greater cosmic renewal (including the rebirth of those who had died) that was to come some time in the indefinite future?

2. *Climatic/Solar Cycles.* It did not take much common sense to associate agricultural cycles with climatic cycles. When the sun seemed to die at the end of the year, it seemed that vegetation also died. It appeared that the death and resurrection of agricultural cycles had something to do with the death and resurrection of the sun. For those who thought of the sun as a god, it was evident that the annual death of the sun god brought about the

death of crops. It was through his powerful rays that the sun god brought about the growth of vegetation. When the sun god died each year, when his influence diminished and abated, so also did the hand of decay and decline touch all growing things.

Fortunately, the sun god was reborn each year; in the minds of common folk the sun god arose from the dead on an annual basis. What meaning was attached to the repeated death and resurrection of the sun god by ordinary people in regard to their own possible survival of death? Did the death and resurrection of the sun god each year contribute anything to the shaping of the collective unconscious of the race? I think it did.

3. *Daily Cycles*. The portrayal of the death of the sun god, of course, was a daily occurrence and not something that happened simply on an annual basis. The bright sun was necessary for both warmth and light. The warming rays of the sun energized people and provided them with the wherewithal to work. Work cannot be accomplished by those who shiver against the cold nor by those who cannot see what they are doing. The birth of the sun each morning was welcomed by those who had no guarantee of whether the sun would return again after its descent into the lower regions below the western horizon. Yet each new morning provided a view of a resurrection of sorts when the sun appeared again above the eastern horizon. The demise of the solar disk occurred each night; the rebirth of the sun became manifest each morning. The daily repetition of the disappearance of the sun into the nether world of the west and its reappearance each day in the east must have produced a powerful impact in the unconscious realms of the human psyche and in the memory of the human race.

4. *Stellar Cycles*. One of the great pastimes in the ancient world was the study of the night skies. The night skies were examined not only by sages but by mariners who guided their ships by the stars, by shepherds who passed the night observing familiar patterns of stars, and by other ordinary people who stood in awe of the majestic vault of the heavens. The night sky, of course, was much more familiar to ancient peoples than it is to individuals today. Observers could readily see in their visual range the decline and advent of constellations and planets at different seasons and at different times during the night.

A constellation is a configuration of relatively bright stars based on imaginary figures. In the ancient Western world there were 47 constellations; the imaginary figures for which the constellations were named came largely from Greek and Roman mythology. What ancient stargazers saw when they looked to the night skies were usually not individual stars but constellations. Thus, they would see not simply a mass of bright stars, but the figure of, say, the princess Andromeda who was rescued from a monster by Perseus. These representations of mythological characters would come and go during the course of a night. Their comings and goings were also dependent on seasonality and on the point of reference of the viewer under the starry canopy. At a particular season Andromeda departs from the scene in the night sky but reappears again the next night. What fades into absence one night comes in view the next night.

The important notion here concerns the continuing departure of a constellation and its continuing return. The cycles of demise and rebirth manifested in astronomical phenomena are perhaps not as dramatic as the cyclic death and resurrection of the sun, i.e., the sun god, during the course of the year. Nonetheless the pattern of going and coming of constellations would fit well with the patterns of death and resurrection manifested elsewhere in human experience.

5. *Sleep and Wakedness.* Perhaps nothing other than sleep is more appropriately compared with death. We lose consciousness in sleep; we lose our conscious selves in a world of dreams. Similarly, nothing other than awaking from sleep is analogous to a rebirth or renewal. Death itself has often been compared to sleep not only in literature but in ordinary speech. Likewise sleep is sometimes said to be a rehearsal for death. During thousands of years this pattern of losing oneself in sleep and gaining a refreshed self upon awakening has been an essential component of shared human experience. Each separate cycle of falling asleep and rising to a wakened state reinforced the image of death and resurrection in the collective unconscious.

6. *The Wax and Wane of Tribal Fortunes.* Every tribe and community experienced on a periodic basis times of good and bad fortune. A particular community might chant songs of lamentation around the campfires because of a failure of the hunt or a poor harvest. Durations of drought or pestilence would sorely try the hope of ancient peoples. Defeat in conflicts with other tribes or communities would have weighed heavily on the minds of every member of the tribe or community. At times the future of an entire village may have been threatened. The people were haunted by specters of future doom; the death and dissolution of the village may have appeared imminent.

Then, some sudden good fortune visited the people: success in the hunt or harvest, a refreshing rainfall and return to health, or a victory against a competing tribe. Hope would be rewarded as a glorious vision of the people's future took shape. A situation that was once adverse now became promising. Elders of the tribe or community, having lived through various challenges to the very existence of the people, might begin to think in terms of patterns of danger and reward, peril and survival, and decrease and increase as normally-occurring patterns of life. This sense of defeat and victory as a prevailing motif was, of course, reinforced by other experiences noted above, e.g., the daily victory of the sun out of the darkness of the night.

7. *Mood Cycles.* Gerald Slusser observed that the "dynamic relationships of archetypes within the psyche produce the particular state of the psyche at any given moment and thus are the basis of any interaction with entities beyond the psyche, e.g., the environment. This dynamic state of the psyche might be called its mood." [20] He goes on to write that the philosopher Martin Heidegger advised a comparable use of this notion. Our mood at any particular moment is a way of being-in-the-world. Human moods change. Depending on the interaction of a person with the external environment, his or her mood may be ascendent or descendent. That is, given a particular situation someone might be very happy or very sad. Sometimes the change of mood from glad to sad or vice-versa has little to do with the external environment and much to do with the internal association of archetypes, with diet, with the need for sleep, with the focus of attention on a happy or melancholy memory, or with a host of all of these and other factors not named here.

The rate of change of moods is variable within the human population. The moods of some individuals change quickly while the moods of others take more time to change. The span of the change of moods is also variable. One person may be quite even tempered in most circumstances; another person's moods swing from high peaks of joy to deep valleys of gloom.

In some mood changes—in some ways of being-in-the-world—an individual may experience a psychic taste of death in feelings of despondency, melancholy, or woe. The same individual may also experience a psychic taste of renewal due to a particular interaction of ideas and images in the individual or collective unconscious, particularly in the encounter of another human whose presence in the world promises friendship. This taste of renewal may well be compared to a sense of one's deliverance from the belly of the beast, a sense of one's own resurrection. These experiences of mood changes—these changes of one's sense of being-in-the-world—enable human beings to gain some limited affective experience of what it could be like to die and what it could be like to arise again in the land of the living.

Archetypes: Cyclic or Linear Time?

A brief parenthesis is needed here. This excursus concerns the conceptualization of history and time as either cyclical or linear. Is there an archetype of the collective unconscious—generated by the universal human experience of death/resurrection in the natural order of creation—that suggests whether time flows in a circle always repeating itself or in a straight line ordered toward some final resolution or Point Omega?

It is in the interaction of unconscious meaning structures among themselves and with the external environment that new meaning structures or archetypes are constructed. In the experience of cycles of death and rebirth in almost every aspect of human life, as noted above, it was quite possible to apprehend the cycles as paradigmatic for the world and for human events. The notion of reincarnation and the cyclic idea of history wherein everything repeats itself over and over again—the myth of the eternal return—probably emerged out of the archetypes of the collective unconscious and formed the basis for philosophies/religions of eternal return. Mircea Eliade observes that when cyclic time becomes desacralized and having no religious implications, "cyclic time becomes terrifying; it is seen as a circle forever turning on itself, repeating itself to infinity." [21]

The *cyclicism* of the experience of the departure/return theme seemingly implicit in vegetation, astronomical phenomena, sleep and awakedness, the fortunes of the tribe, and mood changes could serve as a basis for the development of the myth of eternal return and/or doctrines of reincarnation. This, in fact, is what actually occurred largely outside of the Judaeo-Christian tradition. Within the Judaeo-Christian tradition, perhaps with some dependence on Persian religions, there developed the momentous idea of history as linear and time as an arrow directed toward some denouement. History did not repeat itself *ad infinitum*. On the contrary, history and time were headed, for the Jews, toward the Day of Yahweh and the arrival of the Messiah and, for the Christians, the Day of Yahweh conceived as Final Judgment when the Messiah will return again.

The cyclicism of the experience of the departure/return theme in human experience was ignored in the Judaeo-Christian tradition in favor of a linear interpretation of departure/return, i.e., the sun descends into the west every night and arises again in the east every day as individual iterations of the message of nature. The message is not one of eternal return but of death and resurrection, a message repeated again and again as if to express the importance of its content. I suggest that the ideas/images of cyclic time and, later, linear time both originated initially in the archetypes of the collective unconscious and were subsequently developed when these ideas/images were brought to focused consciousness.

Revival Myths as Proleptic

Meaning structures of hope and renewal became present in the collective unconscious of the race as a result of the universal human experience of the theme of death/resurrection in nature. These archetypes grounded the stories of great heroes (probably actual historical figures) who were celebrated for their mighty deeds. Myths or embellished traditions identified these heroes as somehow overcoming death and undergoing a marvelous awakening. These myths, in their own way, prepared the way for the message of Jesus' resurrection from the dead. The myths that presented heroes and deities as overcoming death were proleptic accounts in regard to the resurrection of Jesus.

The word prolepsis is attributed to anything that represents a future event as if the future event had already taken place. The stories of Attis, Adonis, Hyacinth, Osiris, and other dying and reviving gods can be understood in the great scheme of things only by recognizing the celebration of these myths prior to the Christian message as anticipating, in a highly ambiguous but undeniable manner, the resurrection of Jesus. Pagan revival myths, it can be effectively argued, do not explain the resurrection of Jesus as "just another myth." On the contrary, for the Christian faithful (and perhaps even those who are not Christian but whose hearts are open to the Christian message) the resurrection of Jesus ultimately explains the meaning of pagan myths. Myths of dying and reviving gods were conscious expressions of the resurrection archetype within the collective unconscious. The myths were products of the meaning structures which took form from the common human experiences of the death and resurrection theme manifested in the natural world. The resurrection of Jesus, on the other hand, was a proclamation of a mighty deed of God in human history, a deed that was in itself the actual fulfillment of the myths and authentication of the resurrection archetype.

The recitation of the myths of Attis, Adonis, and other heroes, and the ritual enactments of these myths, prepared the minds and imaginations of millions of people for the Christian message. While elements of these myths departed from the truth and were sometimes morally disreputable, the core meaning of the myths served the cause of Jesus Christ. When pagan resurrection myths were celebrated they pointed obscurely to the future key event, the resurrection of Jesus, that served to validate whatever degree of truth borne by the myths.

The Faith Response to the Good News

In the *City of God*, St. Augustine of Hippo addresses the issue of the credibility of the Christian doctrine of the bodily resurrection of Jesus from the dead. The saint developed an interesting argument: Even if we grant that the resurrection of the body was once beyond belief, the "whole world now believes that the earthly body of Christ has been taken up to heaven." [22] (His argument has merit even when we allow the "whole world" does not believe in the resurrection of Jesus. Millions of Christians do believe and that satisfies the requirements of the argument). In the face of this we are confronted with some interesting choices.

If Christians believe *because* the resurrection is credible, the incredulous need to ask themselves why they continue to find it difficult to believe. If millions of Christians believe *despite* the incredibility of the teaching, how explain that so many could be so wrong? What is it about those believing Christians that elicits their belief? Are all Christians to be written off as mad or stupid? Surely the fact that hundreds of millions would believe in the resurrection is a miracle in itself.

What actually made the resurrection of Jesus credible to the early Christians and to all who have heard and accepted the good news of Jesus' resurrection was not only what occurred *objectively* (the preaching and witnessing of the apostles, martyrs, apologists, and their successors) and was present to the consciousness of believers, but also something far more subtle. Pagan resurrection myths accustomed the consciousness of early converts to Christianity to the idea and image of the resurrection, but the faith response of those who believed in the resurrection of Jesus was also made possible in another way.

What I have called the resurrection archetype, the primal meaning structure impressed on the collective unconscious of the race by ongoing experiences of the "death and resurrection" in nature, influenced hearers of the good news *subjectively* and *unconsciously* to affirm the heralding of Jesus' resurrection as something eminently credible. This is not to say that the resurrection archetype compelled those who heard the good news of Jesus to an affirmative faith response. The force of action of the collective unconscious must be compared to a hint or insinuation instead of an order or command. It must also be noted that the contents of the *individual* unconscious and the process of *individual* consciousness ordinarily functioned with the resurrection archetype in the *collective* unconscious to forestructure the understanding of those who heard the Christian message in such a manner that they would be receptive to this message. Nor do I wish to leave the power of the Holy Spirit out of the interpretation of how and why the resurrection of Jesus seemed credible to believers. The chief focus of my present concern, however, is the dynamic of the resurrection archetype.

When many people heard the Christian message for the first time, they were inspired by the ideas/images in the resurrection archetype to affirm the message they heard. Under the guidance of the promptings from the resurrection archetype they might say to themselves (if this process was conscious): "Yes, the announcement of the resurrection of Jesus is entirely congenial with everything I know and feel about the world in which I live. To believe in the resurrection of Jesus is in accord with what I have sensed all of my life. The resurrection of Jesus is worthy of belief." The resurrection of Jesus from the dead, far from posing credibility problems for potential believers, fit the anticipations of a primary psychic meaning structure far more than even St. Augustine knew.

Concluding Remarks

Professor A. Wilder reported that a speaker at a conference accepted both God and morality but was disaffected from the doctrine of the resurrection. "Resurrection was felt to be too massively involved in the ancient structures of imagination and thinking to be 'demythologized.'" [23] It may be possible, I suggest, to accept the resurrection of Jesus as a mere symbol that evokes personal religious responses but not as a definite presence (whatever the precise nature of this presence) of the risen Jesus to his disciples. It is possible to interpret the testimony of the apostles about the risen Jesus as a plain fable and continue to find something worthwhile in Christianity; but a faith based on the denial of Jesus' resurrection and a series of mental acrobatics to justify that faith as precisely Christian, I argue, is more of a faith in modernist dogmas than in Jesus the Lord. What is common, perhaps, to many who write about the Jesus of history, beyond their concerns for methodology, is their inability to accept the possibilities of occurrences outside of narrowly defined interpretive categories. Their interpretive categories and principles, in turn, are founded on prejudices hostile to supernatural religion. These prejudices are derived from Enlightenment animosities to any religion beyond the natural religion congenial to Deism. These prejudices include the bias against any experience of the "uncanny" or the *mysterium tremens et fascinans* associated with the sense of the Holy, a bias that rules out any appeal to transcendence. Everything must be reduced to the commonplace, to what is prosaic and explicable in terms of natural causes only. Everything marvelous, it seems, must be explained away. This is why it becomes necessary to explain away the bodily resurrection of Jesus as a mere fabrication or fanciful doctrine.

The resurrection of Jesus may indeed be unacceptable to some persons because it is redolent of ancient, pre-Enlightenment structures of imagination and thinking. The resurrection of Jesus would be unacceptable to many of us, however, if it was not redolent of ancient structures of imagination and thinking. The same God who raised Jesus from the dead is the God who created the ancient structures of imagination and thinking. Primal meaning structures are what make human beings authentically human. To reject these meaning structures or archetypes is to begin to deny not only our continuity with the past but the common experiences of our race concerning the great theme of death and resurrection that is written in the everyday processes of the natural world.

Notes to Chapter 3

1. Gerald O'Collins observes that the Deist assumptions of some contemporary theological revisionists prevent them from acknowledging Jesus as truly revealing purposes for us. "If we think of God after creation as having simply left the universe on automatic pilot, we cannot then turn around and recognize Jesus (or anyone else for that matter) as someone through whom God deals with us in new and special ways." "What They Are Saying About Jesus Now," *America,* 171, 5, (1994), 13.
2. Paul Veyne, *Did the Greeks Believe in Their Myths?: An Essay on the Constitutive Imagination,* trans. Paula Wissing, (Chicago: University of Chicago Press, 1988), 62.
3. Ibid., 62.
4. Lawrence Hatab, *Myth and Philosophy: A Contest of Truths* (LaSalle, IL: Open Court, 1990), xi.
5. Ibid., 8.
6. Ibid., 23.
7. Justin Martyr. "The First Apology of Justin," trans. & ed.Alexander Roberts and James Donaldson. *The Ante-Nicene Fathers* (Edinburgh, Scotland: T. & T. Clark, 1993), 170. Justin's work was written about 160 A.D. One of the best contemporary reviews of myth vis-a-vis the Christian message is Donald Bloesch's "The Bible and Myth," *Christian Foundations: Holy Scripture* (Downers Grove: InterVarsity Press, 1994), 255–277.
8. Ibid., 181.
9. Carl G. Jung, *The Structure and Dynamics of the Psyche,* trans. R.F. Hull (New York: Pantheon Books, 1960). 133.
10. Ibid., 133.
11. Carl G. Jung, *Two Essays on Analytical Psychology,* trans. R. F. Hull (Princeton: Princeton University Press, 1977), 65.
12. Carl G. Jung, *Four Archetypes,* trans. R. F. Hull (Princeton: University of Princeton Press, 1992), 48.
13. Carl G. Jung, *C.. G. Jung: Letters,* trans. R. F. Hull (Princeton: University of Princeton Press, 1975), 275. If one "knows" something, of course, it is not necessary to believe.
14. Blaise Pascal, *Penses,* trans. A. Krailsheimer (London: Penguin Books, 1966), 154.
15. See Anthony Kenney, *What is Faith?* (New York: Oxford University Press, 1992), 89–109. Kenny admirably presents Newman's ideas on the faith in the essay "John Henry Newman on the Justification of Faith." Also, an obediential potency may be considered a power an individual has that enables that person to respond affirmatively to the revealing word of God.
16. Joseph Campbell, *The Hero with a Thousand Faces* (Princeton NJ: Princeton University Press, 1968), 30–40.
17. Joseph Campbell, *The Inner Reaches of Outer Space* (New York: HarperPerennial, 1986), 11–12.
18. James Frazer, *The Golden Bough: A Study of Magic and Religion* (Hertfordshire, UK: Wordsworth Editions, 1993), 325.

19. Mircea Eliade, *A History of Religious Ideas:From Stone Age to Eleusinian Mysteries*, trans. Willard Trask (Chicago: University of Chicago Press, 1978), 40.
20. Gerald Slusser, *From Jung to Jesus: Myth and Consciousness in the New Testament* (Atlanta, GA: John Knox Press, 1986), 33.
21. Mircea Eliade, *The Sacred and the Profane*, trans. Willard Trask (New York: Harper and Brothers, Harper Torchbook, 1961), 107.
22. Augustine of Hippo, *City of God*, trans. G. Walsh, D. Zema, G. Monahan and D. Honana (New York: Doubleday Image Books, 1958), 505–508.
23. A. Wilder, *Theopoetic: Theology and the Religious Imagination* (Philadelphia: Fortress Press, 1976), 3–4

4

RESURRECTION FAITH
AND IMAGINATION

Some people have no difficulty professing faith in the resurrection of Jesus. Others find it troublesome to assent to this central message of the Christian faith. Why? There is a close and significant relationship, I submit, between the condition of a person's imagination and his or her response to the proclamation of the bodily resurrection of Jesus. Sometimes it is neither an imperfection of intelligence nor a moral flaw that hinders an individual from a faithful response, but instead an imagination simply lacking the capacity for resurrection faith. This lack of capacity is a deficiency that grows out of an imagination that places arbitrary limits on the idea of the *possible*. What supports religious belief in general, and faith in the resurrection in particular, is an adequately cultivated imagination founded on the controlling principle that all things are possible with God.

The power of imagination originates within anyone's overall conception of what the world is actually like. When an individual is presented with an ambiguous situation, a situation that is open to many different interpretations, the interpretation which finally wins out is usually the one that corresponds most closely with the person's internal image of the world. The existence of diverse interpretations of texts or life events (which can be thought of as text analogues) points to the prevalence of much ambiguity in the world we share. This is particularly true about religious belief in the modern era.

Suppose three individuals read the text of Paul's first letter to the Corinthians on the resurrection of Jesus (1 Cor 15). The first person believes that Jesus was raised bodily from the dead; the second person believes that the text refers to a symbolic resurrection that presents some profound religious truth but not an actual bodily resurrection from the dead; the third person believes that the entire topic of resurrection is full of superstition and nonsense. The imaginations of all three are involved in their respective interpretations of the message. What is clear to one person is not at all clear to the other two. What is congruous with one person's internal image of the real world does not correspond with the internal images of the others. Now what is true for the interpretation of texts is also true for the interpretation of events.[1] This is why there is a plurality of interpretations of a single text or a single event. Each of three differing interpretations of 1 Corinthians 15 is due in large measure to the differences that obtain within the imaginations of the three individuals.

This chapter concerns the place of imagination in the interpretive process relative to Jesus' resurrection. Three considerations are addressed. First, an attempt is made to answer the question "What is imagination?" The response to this question involves: 1) a working definition of imagination, 2) some observations about the relationship between imagination and other mental capacities, and 3) an explanation of the paradigmatic imagination, i.e., the imagination that provides someone with a definite pattern or standard for interpreting the world at large or any aspect of the world.

The second major consideration concerns a brief history of how the modern secular imagination has been shaped during the course of the previous four centuries. The notion of secular is used in the present context in the sense that nothing is deemed possible other than this world, i.e., the possibility of any transcendent reality is denied. The ideological movements of rationalism, scientism, naturalism, materialism, atheism, and nihilism have both contributed to, and reflect, a cultural and intellectual milieu in Western civilization that is hugely inimical to the Judaeo-Christian tradition and antagonistic to the development of any kind of imagination receptive to religious beliefs relative to a supernatural order.

The final part of the chapter relates to the issue of gaining perspective on the modern secular imagination to see how it affects one's own beliefs. It is necessary to understand the biases and prejudices that condition one's own interpretation of the world. It is equally helpful to gain insight into the impact of the secular humanism that enjoys currency in contemporary society. One of the ways of countering the modern secular imagination is a critique of the ideologies which ground this kind of imagination. What is needed in respect to this critique is the ability to think in terms of post-modernity.

The notion of postmodernity was intially proposed as an architectural style that rejected contemporary versions of modernist design, e.g., the large all-glass buildings that filled the skylines of American cities in the post-World War II period. Postmodernity not only rejected modernistic design but attempted to retrieve elements of styles previous to the modern period including even classical design.

Today, there are understandings of postmodernity that are relevant to different areas of human concern and a variety of fields of study. The concept is revisited later in the chapter. It is sufficient to note presently that postmodernity is construed here as a perspective in time and culture that permits a critical evaluative scanning of intellectual history since the 16th century. Prior to the dawning of the postmodern period, the full features of modern ideologies could not be examined in their fullest.

Finally, the modern secular imagination is viewed in a positive light as the source of multiple innovations during the previous three centuries and particularly during the past 100 years. Modern science learned early to look for causes and relationships in this world and not rely on labored explanations that brought in God as a element in scientific equations. This enabled scientists to understand how things worked and how to manipulate physical, chemical, biological, and other mechanisms and organisms to produce a world that is more friendly, at least in developed nations, to the people. Science, technology, and engineering have wrought wonderous things, inventions, and discoveries that have broadened the imagination considerably. This has taught many not to limit unnecessarily their definitions of what is possible.

What is Imagination?

What philosophers have said and written about imagination over the course of the previous 2300 years is extremely complicated. Imagination has been defined basically as the power of making mental images. These images are different from sense perceptions but depend nonetheless on the senses as they relate to cognition or knowledge. From Plato to Kant some philosophers maintained that imagination contributes to knowledge while others warned that imagination was dangerous to reason. Immanuel Kant maintained there were two inter-related kinds of imagination. First, the imagination that completes fragmentary sensory data, e.g., someone has only a partial view of a friend at a distance but is able to reconstruct from memory, by the power of imagination, the image of the entire person in such a manner that identification of the friend is possible on the basis of fragmentary data. This reproductive kind of imagination helps us form the whole from only partial sensory information.

The productive imagination, on the other hand, constructs a synthesis of all of our experience. This makes a coherent experience of the world possible.[2] This coherent experience of the world may properly be called a worldview, a mental image of the world. A worldview, defined for present purposes, is an imaginary depiction of what the world is like and how the world operates. Note well, the term imaginary in the previous sentence should not be construed as denoting something unreal, fictional, or purely fanciful. What is imaginary can be fictional and fanciful, but it need not be. Images produced by the imagination can be checked against critical norms of what is actual and/or what is possible.

Imagination: A Definition

Mary Warnock, in her classic work entitled simply *Imagination,* takes an insight from Kant's notion of the productive imagination and defines imagination as "our means of interpreting the world."[3] We form images of the world in our minds interpretively by means of imagination. These images are contained within the interpretations that result from the interpretive process. Imagination provides us with the wherewithal to go beyond sense perception into the world of thought. Warnock goes on to observe that imagination is a power of the mind "which is at work in our everyday perception of the world, and is also at work in our thoughts about what is absent." This power makes it possible for us to see the world, whether parts of it are present or absent, as significant. Finally, the power of imagination "is not only intellectual. Its impetus comes from the emotions as much as from the reason, from the heart as much as from the head."

Imagination and Other Human Capacities

Some persons are accustomed to thinking of various mental operations as "faculties" of the mind. Cognition is the faculty by which we know, volition is the faculty by which we choose, emotion is the faculty by which we experience affect, etc. In this scheme, imagination would be the faculty by which we form mental images.

There is a warrant to speak of these capacities as essentially distinct because the infinitives to know, to feel, to choose, and so forth suggest operations that are essentially different. However, we must not fall into error of supposing operations which are notionally distinct are necessarily existentially separate. The human mind is not actually segmented into different pigeonholes that contain various powers. Imagination is not a separate faculty of mind but a capacity that touches all mental powers.

Knowing, feeling, choosing, doing, thinking, and imagining are interpenetrative processes united within the person who undertakes some human task. All human capacities feed into everyone's interpretations of the world. When someone reasons in an attempt to solve a problem, a number of mental capacities work together in harmony, e.g., the person's *choice* to proceed and continue in problem solving, an *understanding* of similar problems which provides background information, a *sense of appropriateness* that guides steps in the problem-solving procedure, the individual's *dominant mood*, and his or her *imagination* work together in harmony. All mental capacities, it seems to me, refer one to another when someone thinks. If any one of these mental powers is absent or substantially retarded in someone, the outcomes of that person's mental activities will be something less than optimum. Visualize, please, a person who lacks all feeling and imagination, and relies rigidly only on cold logic, someone who resembles a Mr. Spock of the celebrated *Star Trek* television episodes and movies. Such a person is more like a computer than a human being. The decisions of this person would follow only one simplistic model of rationality, and would lack spontaneity and creativity. Mr. Spock would have far less to offer at a picnic or party than on a tour of outer space.

A final note about the product of imagination is necessary. Imagination must be confused neither with perception nor ideation. The notion of the image produced by the imagination, as the notion is employed here, is neither a percept nor a concept. It is, perhaps on many occasions, something that combines both perceptual and conceptual elements. The imagination's image is an idea-image: something less than a full-blown idea and something more than an ordinary percept. The product of imagination straddles the difference between particularity and universality, between concreteness and abstractness. This idea-image is the consequence of the joint work of the mind's perceptual and conceptual apparata. Edward Casey writes that "imaginative presentations may in fact serve to *supplement* perceptual presentations."[6] I may hear someone mention the notion of education in general (concept); I decide to associate this notion in my imagination with the brick school house of my youth (percept). Imaginative presentations may serve to embellish abstract concepts. Another example is more relevant to the topic of this book: I may view a picture of the crucifixion of Jesus and, in my imagination, blend this percept with some theological idea of redemption. Or, I may read about redemption as a concept and adorn this concept in my imagination with an image of Jesus' suffering, death, and resurrection. Imagination is a bridge between percept and concept, a bridge that bears the load of the judgments we make.

The Paradigmatic Imagination

According to Garrett Green, in his important book *Imagining God: Theology and the Religious Imagination,* the "paradigmatic imagination is the ability to see one thing *as* another."[7] That is, someone is able to see a reality as something other than what it appears to be in the light of a governing framework or paradigm. The Christian paradigmatic imagination, for example, permits an individual Christian to see the world *as* the handiwork of God. Of course, everyone does not possess the same sort of imagination. Each person's imagination operates out of a specific paradigm that permits the imagination to interpret the world in accordance with the contours of the paradigm. The paradigm holds distinctive beliefs and values, and is constructed largely on the basis of each individual's experiences.

Earlier the beliefs of three people regarding the resurrection were contrasted. The first person believes that Jesus was raised bodily from the dead. The governing paradigm of this individual might be called the traditional Christian paradigmatic imagination. The second individual believes that the resurrection is a symbolic story that denotes a religious truth. The interpretive paradigm of the imagination in this instance could be called a liberal Protestant paradigm. Finally, the paradigm that rules the imagination of the third person—the one who believes any talk of a resurrection is nonsense—might be called a modern secular paradigm.

A Christian paradigmatic imagination makes possible a "seeing" or interpreting of the world relative to a body of Christian teaching and praxis. Not every Christian, however, interprets the world in exactly the same way. This is due to the fact that the unique life experiences of various Christians shape their paradigmatic imaginations somewhat differently. A group of Christians representing various traditions may recite the Apostles' Creed together and mean every word they say. Because they bring different experiences to the situation, however, their interpretations of the creed may differ to greater or lesser extents. It is not only possible but very likely that a single paradigm may contain a number of subsets. It is also likely that a group of persons who worship together within the embrace of the same Christian tradition may interpret the Apostles' Creed somewhat differently because of their different life experiences. This is why it is possible for some Roman Catholics, for example, to be closer to the Anglican paradigmatic imagination than are some Anglicans, and vice versa. If anyone's interpretation of the particular tradition to which he or she belongs diverges *substantively* from the general established interpretation, that individual may seek to change the general doctrine or join formally a different religious tradition.

The paradigmatic imagination, I suggest, is not solely a product of one's life experiences in the sense of passive experiences, i.e., the events that someone encounters without much reflection as he or she moves through the lifespan. Events that merely occur around someone are necessary but not sufficient to explain the development of a paradigmatic imagination. The mere witnessing of an event without reflection on that event is a marginal experience at best. Random experiential learning—superficial learning of which one is peripherally aware—contributes only minimally at best to the development of the paradigmatic imagination. There is some experiential learning, however, that influences the development of the imagination in subtle and powerful ways. This learning occurs when an individual imbibes uncritically the dominant culture in which he or she lives. A person's paradigmatic imagination can develop by default. That is, someone can become so imbued with regnant cultural values that the person's imagination is at odds with professed or voiced beliefs and values.

The kind of life experience that contributes maximally to the development of any paradigmatic imagination is found in the event with which a person wrestles critically and profoundly. There are certain salient events in everyone's life that require critical analysis. Other significant events are those that touch someone's heart deeply. The events that involve someone's attention, reflection, and feelings are more likely to impact the formation of the paradigmatic imagination than events that simply attract passing notice.

It is possible, perhaps, that at a particular point in life the development of a person's paradigmatic imagination slows or, for all practical purposes, stops altogether. To say that one's paradigmatic imagination has stopped developing is to state equivalently that learning has stopped—a truly unfortunate situation. On the other hand, it is possible to cultivate a paradigmatic imagination whether the paradigm is identified as Marxist, Republican, Islamic, feminist, Jungian, or something else. For a Christian this cultivation of imagination may include prayer, reading the Bible, worship, associating with other Christians, leading a life that instantiates Christian virtues, attending religious education programs, and so forth.

I would also suggest for the cultivation of a Christian imagination the pursuit of learning that is not explicitly religious. To paraphrase an ancient adage, nothing authentically human is alien to the Christian imagination. Any kind of worthwhile "secular" learning can contribute to the ideal development of the Christian paradigmatic imagination. While the Christian imagination cannot be secular as the term is used in this context, the Christian imagination requires a healthy concern for this world, i.e., it requires a healthy degree of secularity. Conversations with others who interpret the world differently can be occasions that enrich someone's paradigm.

The paradigmatic imagination should not be narrowly and restrictively focused on a particular theme. I have met individuals for whom the focus of their entire lives is sports. They think of nothing else. All of their conversation concerns whether or not a basketball or football team will have a winning season. Their paradigms are crabbed, stunted, and fixated on trivial matters. Paradigmatic imaginations can also become pathological. A paradigmatic imagination is pathological when it permits someone to "see" interpretively something that is unreal *as* real or to interpret something monstrously evil *as* morally good. One can think only of Adolf Hitler and his extermination of millions of people as a prime example of a pathological imagination. Even some paradigmatic religious imaginations can abet illusions and warped moral senses. The religious imagination, if not cultivated properly, can decay into an imagination that sponsors the worst kind of fanaticism. The self appraisal of one's own paradigm, then, is of utmost importance for everyone.

If the Christian paradigmatic imagination can change for the better, it can also change for the worse. The thesis elaborated in this chapter is that during the course of the previous 300 years the religious imaginations of millions of people have been influenced negatively by what I style the modern secular imagination.

The Modern Secular Imagination

Dennis Nineham suggests that the great religious difficulty today is not a metaphysical difficulty: "Where men seem to need help above all is at the level of the *imagination;* they need some way of envisaging realities such as God, creation, and providence imaginatively, in a way which does no violence to the rest of what they know to be true."[8] Another way to say this is that the modern secular imagination has displaced the traditional religious imagination and blocked the development of a contemporary religious imagination. The modern secular imagination has supplanted the fundamental religious imagination that has been shared for hundreds, and even thousands, of years by people of different religious heritages.

The Religious Imagination

According to Mary Warnock the loss of the religious imagination in our times is really a loss of joy. "The loss...is the loss of the ability to see *through* objects in the natural world to what lies behind them. For the joyless, each thing is what it is and it suggests nothing further, no intimations of immortality or infinity."[9] By means of the religious imagination believers interpret the things of this world, and the world at large, as signs or symbols of another dimension of reality. The religious imagination "binds back" (*re+ligare* = to bind back, to reconnect) or interpretively rejoins the natural world to the God who made it. The religious imagination not only permits us to "see through" the sign-things that point to God; we are able also to access the transcendent dimension of reality by means of hearing, taste, touch, and the sense of smell. All sensible things, all objects in the world and the world considered as a whole, can be interpreted by the religious imagination as conveying a momentous message: "I am not responsible for my own being; look beyond! I am God's sacrament: a sign that bears grace."

What has occurred during the previous three hundred years or so, gradually but on a grand scale, has been the diminution of the religious imagination. If changes to the religious imagination involved only peripheral issues, all would be well and good. The social and intellectual changes effected by some Enlightenment dogmas, however, attacked the very essence of the religious imagination. The paradigm of the modern secular imagination evokes a belief that it is impossible to "see through" the world. The world *is* as it appears, a mass of raw fact. "What you see is what you get" is the message of the modern secular imagination. The religious imagination as an interpretive means of constructing a worldview has been widely suppressed by the premises of the modern secular imagination, to wit, the doctrines of narrow rationalism, scientism, naturalism, materialism, atheism, and nihilism. It is not as if the diminution of the religious imagination occurred when religious people went to school and learned these doctrines formally, although this may have happened in some instances. The ideologies of the modern secular imagination, on the contrary, permeated the cultural environment of modern life and accomplished their ends quietly and efficiently.

Genealogy of the Modern Secular Imagination

The genealogy of the modern secular imagination can be traced in terms more positive than the rise of Enlightenment ideologies. This genealogy can be written in reference to multiple historical factors including the origin of modern science and technology, the rise of democratic institutions and freedom of speech in contemporary societies, the critique of a sometimes debased traditional religious imagination that amounted to little more than superstition, and many other elements deriving from the Enlightenment that were in themselves positive developments in the civilizing process of humankind.[10] Such positive developments actually contributed to the cultivation of the religious imagination. Some Enlightenment thought lifted the religious imagination from credulity and superstition. Religious faith generally became better informed through the generation of new knowledge and the improvement of religious learning. The religious imagination today, due to the political freedoms derived from the Enlightenment, serves religious persons well in their quest of religious truth and in the practice of their religion. The Enlightenment, to a great degree, made possible the cultivation of a religious imagination that was cautiously reasonable , self-critical, constructive vis-a-vis the civilizing process, and open to the possible. But there was also a dark side to the Enlightenment.

The dark side of the Enlightenment released ideologies upon the world that have produced the modern secular imagination. Those possessing this kind of imagination find it difficult, if not impossible, to accept the resurrection of Jesus even as a remote possibility. One way to trace the genealogy of the modern secular imagination is to survey briefly the ideologies identified above that represent the philosophical excesses of the Enlightenment. This tracing exercise cannot be exhaustive due to space limitations. Indeed, an entire book could be written detailing the genealogy of the modern secular imagination and the various ideas that contributed to, and mirrored, the gradual development this type of imagination. In the present context we must be content with a sketchbook of ideologies associated with the modern secular imagination.

Ideas Have Consequences

Is it possible that trends in the world of theologians, philosophers, and other intellectuals can contribute, along with other ancillary factors, to the production of an ideological environment that challenges Christian faith and imagination? Without developing a lengthy argument, I advise that ideas have consequences. These ideas, as well as the consequences, are magnified when they are disseminated in widely-circulated materials, and when variations on the same ideological themes enjoy currency over a period of three hundred or more years.

At the beginning of the Enlightenment and thereafter, widely-diffused ideas hostile to religion often became the preferred doctrines of opinion leaders, doctrines that pervaded books and subsequently school systems and universities. In the more recent past, those responsible for films, television programming, editorial content in magazines and papers employed the tenets of a popular secularism in their work. Ideas have consequences whether they are immediately infused into the cultural milieu or work their way gradually into the milieu via mass communications. What has come to be known as secular humanism is another name for the ideas that shaped and promoted the modern secular imagination.

It would be less than thoughtful to assume that most cultural changes occur as a direct result of the teaching of philosophical doctrines. Cultural changes, by and large, take hold and spread as a consequence of public behaviors that are informed by certain ideologies. Narrow rationalism takes hold of a community or nation when people live their lives as narrow rationalists. This is true notwithstanding the fact that many narrow rationalists do not know the definition of narrow rationalism. Public behavior, performance, praxis, deportment, demeanor—call it what you may—produce the stimuli for cultural change according to the ideology that informs this behavior, performance, praxis, and so forth.

Thus, scientism is promoted when people act as if science is able to answer every question asked by human beings; naturalism is advanced when people act as if nothing exists that is transcedent to the world of raw fact; materialism is championed when enough individuals operate as if only material things are valuable; practical atheism—the living of lives as if God does not exist —is more of a trigger of cultural and social change than theoretical atheism; nihilism tears away at the fabric of the social order when enough citizens function as if virtues and values are irrelevant. Nonetheless, the genealogy of the modern secular imagination is best charted by exposing the ideologies that constitute the core of modern secular behaviors notwithstanding the fact that social modeling of particular behaviors is far more responsible for the generation of the modern secular imagination. To understand the ideological infrastructure, however, is to come to grips with the most salient framers of the modern secular imagination.

The modern secular imagination is largely the product of selected ideological thrusts that have dominated Western culture since the 17th century. These thrusts include philosophical positions antithetical to religion and particularly inimical to Christianity. The convergence of these theoretical positions has produced effects in the workaday world; these effects have helped fashion the modern secular imagination. The modern secular imagination is characterized by its excessive celebration of Reason, the enthronement of science as the final arbiter in all contended human issues, the unsubstantiated belief that everything in the world (and the world itself) can be explained by natural causes without recourse to any transcendent agency, the tenet that nothing exists except matter, the radical denial of God's reality, by atheism's kindred doctrines of agnosticism and Deism, and through the saturation of popular culture with a virulent nihilism that attacks all religious values.[11]

Each of the constitutive elements of the modern imagination is discussed below in a brief manner. A small sample of representative writers who have promoted these ideologies is presented not necessarily as "great men" who changed history but as examples of prominent thinkers who were among many giving voice to extremist ideologies. The purpose of these citations is simply to draw out brief descriptions of the ideologies associated with the development of the modern secular imagination.

Rationalism. A denunciation of rationalism does not require a wholesale dismissal of rationality. Some models of rationality are proper and appropriate. Rationalism that is self-critical must be distinguished from naive or narrow rationalism. Narrow rationalists maintain that everything is explicable in terms of human reason. What is usually associated with narrow rationalism is the fundamental assumption that divine revelation in religious matters cannot possibly exist. Further, the measure of all religious issues is the human mind. Narrow rationalism insists that once a foundation for reason is established, human reasoning can produce certain and objective responses to all questions.

Modern rationalism can be traced back hundreds of years in the history of philosophy. More recently in history the pivotal philosopher of rationalism was Rene Descartes (1596-1650). Descartes lived at a time when the treasury of conventional knowledge was undergoing wrenching changes. There is no doubt that Descartes was profoundly shaken by these changes. At the age of 23, Descartes experienced a vision in a series of feverish dreams. The vision that came to him was a vision of the unification of all human knowledge.[12] Descartes interpreted this vision as his destiny. All problems in human knowing were to be transformed into problems that could be addressed with mathematical exactitude.

There was a strong motivation for Descartes' desire. Books were being published in great numbers due to the invention of moveable type in the 15th century. Books and tracts containing a profusion of different views were being desseminated widely. New ideas came upon the scene to challenge old ideas. Explorers had returned from exotic lands with stories about far-flung worlds that contested established ideas of the world. Religious reformations and revolutions brought distress and anxiety to many. Religious wars touched the lives of countless men and women. The Copernican revolution was taking place. Heliocentric cosmological theory had displaced the Ptolemaic worldview. A great wave of insecurity swept over Western civilization. Descartes began his adventure in philosophy for a method that would bring pure and objective truth, and certainty, to a waiting world. He initiated a thirst for certainty in knowledge that became almost pathological.

Descartes understood that sense data were too insecure to serve as a foundation for his system. He discovered such a foundation, however, in his own mind. "I think, therefore I am" became his basic truth, an axiom that grounded his entire philosophical project. For the better part of the next three centuries philosophers embarked on a voyage that attempted to discover and to map out the exact operations of the human mind. It was also during this timespan that philosophers worked out elaborate systems which were alleged to have provided final answers to eternal questions.

The coming of the age of reason was not all bad. During the the next 300 years various philosophers, theologians, and other commentators began to interpret religious issues with much more exactitude. Old religious irrationalities were dismissed deservedly and many needed refinements were inaugurated in the study of scripture, particularly in the areas of textual and historical criticism. Corrupt political regimes, civil and ecclesiastical, were targeted for reform. While the Enlightenment definitely had a dark side, not all was darkness, as noted previously.

At the same time, however, valuable religious traditions were attacked and key Christian teachings were repudiated. A search for pure and objective knowledge in religious matters was begun by a number of writers. Symbolic of the deification of Reason (always spelled with an upper case R) was the festival held in Notre Dame cathedral at the height of the French Revolution. This festival was a defining moment of the Enlightenment. The cathedral was renamed the Temple of Reason. A singer from the Paris Opera, dressed in white, portrayed Liberty and payed homage to the flame of Reason. The scene was a harbinger of things to come in intellectual circles. About 50 years later, in 1843, the Bavarian philosopher and theologian Ludwig Feuerbach wrote *The Essence of Christianity*. The themes of narrow rationalism that echoed in his writing were typical of the rationalistic spirit. The power of human reason was extolled while the notion of divine revelation was denigrated. "There is merely an illusory distinction between divine revelation and so-called human reason or nature—the content of divine revelation is of human origin, for it has proceeded not from God as God, but from God as determined by human reason and human wants... Every revelation is simply a revelation of the nature of Man to existing men." Feuerbach transformed theology into anthropology. His ideas strongly influenced Marx and Engels. Narrow rationalism marched into the 20th century via Marxism and, therefore, abetted the creation of the modern secular imagination.

Rationalism, as a postulate of the modern secular imagination, maintains that pure, objective, and certain knowledge is attained only by means of human reason in the utilization of logic and a suitable method. Whatever falls outside of pure, objective, and certain knowledge is mere speculation. Scientific rationalism is a subset of narrow rationalism. Another 17th century philosopher, Francis Bacon (1562-1626), played a crucial role in the eventual shaping of scientific rationalism and, in turn, the development of the modern secular imagination. He proposed that knowledge arose out of systematic empirical observation. Although others before him, even in the ancient world, had discussed inductive reasoning based on the careful examination of concrete reality, Bacon's influence on his peers was strong. Knowledge came to be viewed *restrictively* as the fruit of a methodical examination of the natural world and not as endless discussions of what the ancients said about the natural world. Bacon must be celebrated at one of the leading figures in the establishment of modern science. He initiated a period, though, in which some scientists exceeded the proper boundaries of science and became practitioners of scientism.

Scientism. Now science must be distinguished from scientism. Science and technology have brought humanity many boons, particularly in their flowering in the 19th and 20th centuries. We can look around us and see the wonders of modern medicine, the marvels of aeronautics, and the great outcomes of laboratory experiments in physics, chemistry, and biology. We employ the technological achievement of modern science everyday. It would be foolish not to be impressed favorably with what they have wrought.

Scientism, on the other hand, is the dogma that positive sciences equal truth in all cases. Scientism is a doctrinaire ideology that masks itself in the guise of science. William Barrett wrote that no sooner had science come into the world in the 17th century than it became dogged by scientism. "Scientism is pseudoscience or misinterpreted science. Its conclusions are sweeping and large, and therefore sometimes pretend to be philosophical."[13] Practitioners of scientism taught that the human animal was nothing but a collection of molecules, that blind chance arranged these molecules to evolve into human animals, and that religious truths were the mere outcomes of vain speculations. The truths of revealed religion lack acceptable status since since they do not result from the systematic examination of the natural world and, therefore, are not truths at all.

Scientism is often practiced by scientists who engage in theoretical speculation that is quite beyond the scope of their respective sciences. Carl Sagan, the noted popularizer of empirical science, has often bootlegged philosophy and metaphysical issues into his discussions of scientific matters. In his essay "A Sunday Sermon" he states that he is often asked by lay people whether he believes in God. This opening permits him to deal with the issue of God's existence. He conducts this task in a remarkably superficial way for an entire chapter. Sagan avers that when people ask him whether he believes in God they are seeking "reassurance that their particular belief system...is consistent with modern science knowledge. Religion has been scarred," he writes, "in its confrontation with science, and many people—but by no means all—are reluctant to accept a body of theological belief that is too obviously in conflict with what else we know."[14]

Sagan continues, in his patented imperious manner, to repeat a few silly stories to repudiate the religious beliefs held by simple folk. This was apparently done in an attempt to repudiate religious belief in general. He tells the story of the Soviet Union's first obital flight. After Uri Gagarin's flight, Krushchev assured the people that the cosmonaut had stumbled on no gods or angels. Krushchev assured everyone that manned orbital flight was not inconsistent with their religious beliefs. The implication here is that the religious belief of Russian peasants is the equivalent of the formal creed of the Russian Orthodox Church. Another case recounted by Sagan concerned an American religious sect that declared the world would end in 1914 and, of course, it did not end. The implication is that all religions are wrong. Again, religious persons formerly believed that the opening of a morning glory was due to God's direct microintervention. "The flower was unable to open by itself. God had to say, 'Hey, flower, open.'"[15] "Because we know something about phototropism and plant hormones," Sagan intones, "we can understand the opening of the morning glory independent of divine microintervention."[16]

While many believers, myself included, believe that God, our provident Father, is *ultimately* responsible for opening the flowers, we also understand the process of phototropism as a *secondary* cause in the opening of flowers. That is, God opens the flowers through the process of phototropism which he also created. Sagan was unable to make this distinction between ultimate and secondary or instrumental causality, perhaps, because he cannot spy a provident Father in his telescopes. Apparently Sagan was also oblivious to the possibilty of different levels of explanation or interpretation. Interpretations can be forthcoming from different perspectives. Two entirely different interpretations of Niagara Falls are the result of providing descriptions from a bridge near the falls, on the one hand, and from a jet airliner that is nearly seven miles above the falls on the other hand. The two descriptions may differ considerably, but are valid given the limiting conditions of any particular point of view. Of course, nothing can be known at all, including the existence of ultimate causes, according to scientific rationalists, unless it is experienced through direct scientific observation. The question of whether God opens the flowers, then, is entirely superfluous.

Sagan refers to the work of Andrew Dickson White (1832-1918), the founder and first president of Cornell University. White's book *The Warfare of Science with Theology in Christendom* is identified as extraordinary by Sagan, a judgment with which I would agree but for different reasons than Sagan's. The thrust of White's 1896 work, when it is analyzed and reduced to its gist is this: God has revealed himself in history through the means of Reason and Science, thereby correcting the errors of religion in general and the erroneous claims of Christianity in particular. Reason, it could be said of White's basic belief, constituted authentic revelation. According to White there was no possibility of attaining the truth until the advent of modern empirical science. White wrote that "...modern science in general has acted powerfully to dissolve away the theories and dogmas of the older theologic interpretation, it has also been active in a reconstruction and recrystallization of truth; and very powerful in this reconstruction have been the evolution doctrines which have grown out of the thought and work of men like Darwin and Spencer."[17] The antagonistic flavor of White's comments about Christianity are obvious.

Naturalism. One of the great naturalists of all times was Charles Darwin (1809- 1882). As a naturalist or field biologist Darwin undertook laborious descriptions and categorizations of what he called "organic beings." He was eminent among scientists as a thorough and systematic cataloguer of what he observed. Darwin, however, found himself caught in a dilemma. In his doctrine of natural selection he went beyond the role of scientific naturalist (field biologist) and took upon himself the role of a philosophical naturalist (an anti-supernaturalist theoretician). Wearing the livery of a scientist who provided descriptions of the physical world, Darwin took upon himself the philosopher's cloak to proffer metaphysical interpretations of the origins of the "organic beings" he studied.

That Darwin sensed a difficulty with natural selection, the doctrine that species come into being on the basis of variations within the species during a lengthy expanse of time, is clear from his defense of natural selection in *The Origin of the Species* . "The preservation of favourable individual variations, and the destruction of those which are injurious, I have called Natural Selection, or the Survival of the Fittest."[18] Darwin wrote that several critics misapphrehended or objected to the term Natural Selection. He argued that natural selection does not induce variability; the term "implies only the preservation of such variations as arise and are beneficial to the being under its conditions of life." On the same page Darwin objected to the criticism that he wrote of natural selection as an active power or Deity when his critics would not object to someone who speaks of the law of gravity in ruling the movements of the planets. What he meant by nature, he wrote, is "only the aggregate action and product of many natural laws, and by laws the sequence of events as ascertained by us."[19] Finally, he noted that once there is greater familiarity with his work, superficial objections to natural selection will be forgotten. This opinion must surely have been penned with a great deal of wishful thinking.

In the last result, Darwin did not formulate a biological theory but instead a philosophical doctrine. Natural selection would not have precipitated problems were it not for the fact that natural selection was interpreted as a theoretical doctrine of ultimate origins. Darwin's depiction of evolution was understood by critics as respecting the origin of the human species even though he played this down in *The Origin of the Species* (1859). It was not until *The Descent of Man* (1876) that he made the direct connection of natural selection to human beings. Since the problem of human origins can be addressed at the level of speculative philosophy (an issue of ultimate causality) as well as at the level of biology (an issue of secondary causality), and since Darwin did not address this distinction adequately, it seemed to many that he was offering a doctrine based on the philosophy of naturalism. What Darwin actually intended is difficult to ascertain. It is more difficult, however, to imagine he was completely naive philosophically, especially under some of the more cogent complaints of many of his critics.

As a scientist Darwin wished to develop his theory of natural selection without recourse to any supernatural agency just as Newton addressed the laws of gravity. However, in an historical context in which the philosophy of naturalism and the rejection of God's intervention in human history was prized and celebrated—combined with the fact that the concept of natural selection was obviously open to a philosophical interpretation—it is not surprising that Darwin's theory was interpreted as implying the world itself was self-dependent and self-explanatory. Likewise, Darwin's writings seemed to repudiate the existence of human souls and immortality. Everything examined by science or known to human beings, according to philosophical naturalism, exists self dependently and requires no further explanation for its existence. The universe is not dependent on a creator, and exists of itself and by itself. No wonder theologians and churchmen came to the defense of traditional religious beliefs. (Some of these defenses, it must be admitted, were wrong-headed and fallacious).

In offering his speculative beliefs about the origin of the species as a strict inference based on his scientific findings, it would not be wrong to recognize Darwin as a practitioner of scientism as well as science. In many ways rationalism, scientism, naturalism, materialism, and atheism overlap and ultimately converge. Darwin is classified as a philosophical naturalist here because naturalism is a dominant notion in his worldview. Many of his disciples today are unrepentant philosophical naturalists.

There is no doubt where Darwinists stand today in the interpretation of the meaning of natural selection. Phillip E. Johnson wrote: "By skillful manipulation of categories and definitions, the Darwinists have established philosophical naturalism as educational orthodoxy in a nation in which the overwhelming majority of people express some form of theistic belief inconsistent with naturalism."[20]

(There is a danger in any critique of Darwin's clumsy philosophical naturalism that the concept of evolution itself will be condemned by religious people in a blanket fashion. There are many practicing Christians today who accept some sort of evolution as a process employed by God in the ongoing creation of the world. These Christians do not see any contradiction between the essential meaning of the creation narratives in the book of Genesis and the possibility of a divinely-guided evolution. I mention this to emphasize that the central issue here is not creation versus evolution, but the ideology of philosophical naturalism that rejects the possibility of any reality beyond the raw facts of the material world).

A brief sampling of the writings of George Santayana (1863-1952), an American philosopher who professed naturalism, provides another taste of naturalism and shows how it dovetails with the ideology of rationalism. "As for the Christian doctrine of judgment," he wrote, "it is something wholly out of relation to empirical facts, it assumes the existence of a supernatural sphere, and is beyond the reach of scientific evidence of any kind."[21] Santayana strenuously opposed not only Christian doctrine, but also spirituality. "That spiritual minds should appeal to the supernatural is not to be wondered at. Few are courageous enough to accept nature as it is, and to build their spiritual house on the hard rock of truth."[22] Santayana's naturalism displayed its narrow rationalistic side in much of his writing: "An oracular morality or revealed religion can hope to support its singular claims only by showing its general conformity to natural reason and its perfect beneficence in the world."[23] Again, the deification of autonomous human reason is obvious in Santayana's insistence that religion must "conform" to his definition of "reason. Santayana's naturalism was robust, hostile to religion, and had a definite bite. He did not suffer those who disagreed with him lightly and at one time he was a very influential opinion maker in America.

The foremost American philosopher of naturalism, John Dewey (1859-1952), expressed his philosophy no less pointedly but was more politic in his dialogue with those with whom he disagreed. Dewey, more than any other American, laid the philosophical foundations of American public schooling and contributed immensely to the advance of the secular humanistic environment of the public schools. Naturalism was, in fact, sometimes referred to as humanism, a naturalism that focused on the betterment of humanity through the propagation of a new "faith."

Dewey's philosophy is presented with great clarity in an essay entitled "What I Believe." The essay was published in 1930. Dewey praised the power of individual experience in the natural world. "Adherence to any body of doctrines and dogmas based upon a specific authority signifies distrust in the power of experience to provide, in its own ongoing movement, the needed principles of belief and action. Faith in its newer sense signifies that experience itself is the sole ultimate authority."[24] Immediately Dewey isolated those who affirm religious teachings as distrustful of their own experience in the natural world. Only those who rely on this experience as the sole authority can be said to practice the faith in its newest, modern sense.

Quite calmly, but no less strongly than Santayana, Dewey mounted an attack on religion. "Religions have been saturated with the supernatural—and the supernatural signifies precisely that which is beyond experience."[25] Religion is cast as an avoidance of responsibility by people who wish, according to Dewey, to escape the confusion and ambiguities of personal experience. In opposition to the traditional religions that play to the weakness of human beings, the new faith created by naturalism is on the horizon. "The method we term 'scientific' forms for the modern man (and a man is not modern merely because he lives in 1930) the sole dependable means of disclosing the realities of existence. It is the sole authentic mode of revelation."[26] Dewey's power of expression and ringing rhetoric won him many followers. Behind this power of expression and rhetoric, however, there existed flaws that relatively few were able to detect. The chief flaw in Dewey's thought is the *a priori* assumption that the human capacity for experience is limited to empirical-positivistic experience.

Naturalism is associated explicitly sometimes with scientism, sometimes with rationalism, and at other times with humanism, the kind of humanism that is today understood in the term "secular humanism."[27] Corliss Lamont wrote that humanism believes in an attitude "toward the universe that considers all forms of the supernatural as myth..."[28] He also described humanism as implying "a world-view in which Nature is everything, in which there is no supernatural and in which man is an integral part of Nature and not separated from it by any sharp cleavage of discontinuity."[29] From this is can be easily inferred that scientism, naturalism, and humanism are associated directly with materialism.

Materialism. As a theory of the constitutive basis of reality, materialism was in recent memory the officially sanctioned philosophy of the former Soviet Union, its political satellites, and the Peoples' Republic of China. Materialism, implicit in Marxism, today receives formal approbation in China at least in lip service. Never in the history of the world were more people exposed to an ideology that denied the legitimacy of religious belief.

Charles Mayer described the three postulates of materialism: 1) The universe has existed from all eternity and everything that happens is the result of purely physical laws; 2) life began in the world simply as a result of natural causes; 3) mind is only an expression of matter. He goes on to observe that there are no transcendent truths and no ultimate purpose to the world. All that exists are material facts.[30] In all liklihood most materialists would agree with Mayer. There are, however, distinctive types of materialism.

Karl Marx, in one of his early writings, *The Holy Family*, claimed there were two major strands of materialism. Mechanical materialism was originated by Descartes (1596-1650) and became associated with issues in empirical science. Matter was granted a life of is own, a life manifested in the motion of matter. The second kind of materialism, according to Marx, began with the English philosopher John Locke (1632-1704). Locke's speculations on the role of the senses in understanding were used by the Frenchman Etienne Condillac (1715-1780) to oppose French metaphysics and theology. Condillac's emphasis on sense experience and the influence of environment on human beings was represented in terms of materialism. Marx quipped that the French took English materialism and civilized it. It was this brand of materialism that led directly to socialism and communism.[31]

It has been suggested that Friedrich Engels, the friend of Marx and his collaborator, was much more interested in materialism as a topic of philosophical speculation. Marx' interest in the notion of materialism extended only to dialectical materialism as a correction to dialectical idealism, that is, the process of history moves forward not in the interactive conflict of ideas but in the clash of the material conditions of life and in the dialectical opposition of capitalists and workers.[32] Marx, I propose, was far more aware of the nuances enfolded in the concept of materialism than many of his contemporaries. For all this, however, his materialism, naturalism, and atheism combined to constitute an ideology that vehemently assailed religion.

In the Western democracies, and particularly in America, theoretical materialism has been little more than a handy ideology for leftist enthusiasts who perch prominently on what they perceive to be the moral high ground and deliver rhetorical incantations against real or imagined oppressors. Particularly on many American college campuses, theoretical materialism is generally a basis for the politics of the far left. Some American theoreticians who are antagonistic to religion build their objections on the foundations of scientism and/or naturalism. I base this judgment on my experience in academia during the previous two decades.

In practice, however, millions of Americans and Europeans have fallen under the sway of a kind of consumerism that belies their vocal dedication to spiritual values. This is often accompanied by a fixation on the "things of this world" to such an extent that religious values seem to have vanished in their daily lives. Christians need to maintain a healthy secularity in respect to the world and an avoidance of the camel syndrome, i.e., a burying of heads in the sand and a total disregard of the world. For Christians, the world should be an object of their concern insofar it cries out for deliverance from evil. Unfortunately, all too often many Christians come under the spell of secularism and act as if there is nothing transcendent to the world. In short, even some Christians (and perhaps these are mainly nominal Christians only) live as if God is truly dead.

Atheism. The last of the historical antecedents of the modern imagination is atheism or the denial of God's existence. I wish to consider the writings of two individuals: Sigmund Freud and the Nobel laureate Francis Crick. Arguably Freud had more influence on the shaping of modern mores than most prominent writers who lived in the 20th century. His depiction of religion as a neurosis has propagated both a negative outlook on religion in our culture and, subsequently, a largescale loss of a sense of God's reality. Francis Crick's ideas are included because of the recency of his writing. Crick, who with James D. Watson determined the structure of DNA, published his latest book in 1994 and takes as his task an argument against the existence of the soul. In the process, his atheism becomes clearly obvious. He lends his stature as a Nobel laureate to the ongoing sustenance of the modern secular imagination.

In the Vienna of 1938 Freud wrote that his "old enemy," the Church, was protecting him from the reach of Hitler's minions. Freud was reluctant to arouse the hostility of his "old enemy." He noted that he would be endangered if his work led to the remembrance of what he had written previously: "If our work leads us to a conclusion which reduces religion to a neurosis of humanity and explains its enormous power in the same way as a neurotic compulsion in...individual patients, we may be sure of drawing down the resentment of the ruling powers. Not that I should have anything to say that would be new or that I did not say clearly a quarter of a century ago."[33] In the same book Freud wrote that his experiences in life made it impossible for him to accept the existence of a Supreme Being, the God of the believers he had met.

Earlier, in 1927, Freud had written *The Future of An Illusion*. The illusion of which he wrote was religion. This illusion is characterized by the belief that life serves a higher purpose, and that over each person "there watches a benevolent Providence... which will not suffer us to to become a plaything of the overmighty and pitiless forces of nature. Death itself is not an extinction, it is not a return to inorganic lifelessness, but the beginning of a new kind of existence..."[34]

Freud also wrote that civilization has little to fear from educated people and brainworkers when comes the time that most people eventually lose their belief in God. In them religious motives for proper behavior would be replaced by secular motives. It is a different story with the uneducated, however since they have every reason to be enemies of civilization with their belief in God. "So long as they do not discover that people no longer believe in God, all is well. But they will discover it, infallibly, even if this piece of writing of mine is not published."[35]

Freud suggests, though, that even the uneducated may possibly learn to get along without God. On the one hand, if the only reason they do not kill one another is belief in a punishing God, they may go on a rampage when they discover there is not a punishing God; on the other hand, the relationship between civilization and religion may be re-established. Although he does not make explicit what the re-establishment of this relationship might be like, there is little doubt religion would become merely an opium of the uneducated masses at the hands of the intellectual elites.

The militancy of Freud's atheism is outstripped only by the vigor with which he equates religious belief with ignorance and miseducation, and by the hubristic elitism that characterizes his comments about the uneducated. Those today who view religious belief as a sure token of naivete are no less aggressive in their opposition to religion. They promote the modern secular imagination in nearly every walk of life and pronounce the modern imagination as alone appropriate for interpretation of the world.

Francis Crick, known for his work with James D. Watson in determining the structure of DNA, has also been known as a strong voice that trumpets religion as a leftover of a bygone era. Science alone, he avers, is the source of true knowledge. While he may be categorized as a philosophical naturalist or a priest of scientism, atheism/agnosticism is also an essential focus of his worldview. In his most recent book (1994) Crick argues against belief in the existence of the soul. The soul, Crick suggests, is common to all religions. In the introduction of the book, Crick recounts an alleged anecdote about the scientist Pierre-Simon Laplace and Napoleon. After Laplace explained the workings of the solar system to Napoleon, the emperor asked what part God played in Laplace's explaination of the solar system. "Sire," replied Laplace, "I have no need of that hypothesis."[36]

Crick emphasizes the same thought that is so explicit in Freud's writing, the belief that educated people today are not religious believers in any true sense of the term. "Many educated people, especially in the Western world, also share the belief that the soul is a metaphor and there is not personal life either before or after death. They may call themselves atheists, agnostics, humanists, or just lapsed believers, but they all deny the major claims of traditional religions."[37]

To a great extent Crick is correct. It is not due to education itself that many find it difficult to believe; it is due, instead, to the fact they have been exposed to an education that uncritically and unrelentingly fashions the modern secular imagination. For those whose imagination is uncritically modern, the claim that Jesus was raised bodily from the dead by his Father in heaven can hardly be taken seriously. This claim cannot be accomodated interpretively due to the constraints of the modern secular imagination. Anyone whose imagination has been infected, for example, with philosophical naturalism will find it impossible to believe in Jesus' resurrection simply because one of the major tenets of naturalism is that there is no dimension of reality transcendent to the natural order we see before us. If there is no transcendent dimension, Jesus could hardly have risen and ascended to his Father in heaven.

Nihilism. Friedrich Nietzsche wrote of the madman who lit a lantern and went searching for God in the market place in the bright morning hours. "I am seeking God," he shouted. Many of those in the market place did not believe in God and they began to mock the madmen. "The madman jumped into their midst and pierced them with his eyes. 'Whither is God?' he cried; 'I will tell you. We have killed him—you and I...God is dead. And we have killed him."[38] Nietzsche ended the story with momentous words from the lips of the madmen. He forced his way into several churches and intoned a requiem for the dead God. The churches, he averred, are little more than the tombs of God.

Nihilism is essentially the negation of all traditional values, particularly the devaluation of what Nietzsche called the "uppermost" values of civilization. Through the will to power, according to Nietzsche, new values come into existence by means of a reevaluation. In proclaiming the death of God, Nietzsche was issuing a warning to people that they were about to be visited by the dissolution of all they held dear and that they should strive to create new values and patterns for exemplary human existence by exercising the will to power. Nietzsche is sometimes hailed as a prophet and a guide to a new way of being human. This new way of being human would lead eventually to a new order where all people would become equal through the exercise of their will to power. Until then, however, we live in the fog of pessimism because with the death of God comes the death of all values.

What is problematic about the Nietzschean worldview in which a new order is celebrated is that it is much easier to tear things down than to rebuild. It is doubtful, at best, that millions of individuals all exerting their will to power will be able to construct anything more than a new tower of Babel. Nietzsche lived from 1844 to 1900. Some of what he wrote was grossly misunderstood in popular writings. Nonetheless, it is arguable whether his philosophy, rightly or wrongly understood, is connected to some of the most evil events of the 20th century.

In the meanwhile, we are indeed living in the midst of the dissolution of values. As we move toward the 21st century, moral anarchy seems at hand, the kind of anarchy that is a harbinger of possible political anarchy. God is dead not in the sense that he has actually died, but in the figurative sense of being absent by the choice of those who should adore him. God is simply ignored. God, and the values founded in God, are simply a matter of colossal indifferance. Look around at the world in which we live: We have been visited by moral dissolution. Sickness of the soul is everywhere and everywhere people are dying spiritually. The modern secular imagination is far worse off due to nihilism—the condition is which nothing matters and there is no purpose to life—than to atheism. The atheist, at least, takes the idea of God seriously enough to mount an argument against God. The nihilist merely reads the obituaries of God that are seemingly posted everywhere in our culture, and exerts his or her will to power in pursuit of baubles and ashes.

If someone is convinced that there is no purpose or meaning in life, it is clear that that person's religious imagination will be shriveled and weak. Living as if nothing matters and in the grip of pessimism shapes and feeds the modern secular imagination.

The Modern Secular Imagination: A Postmodern Critique

Many people can become receptive to the announcement of the resurrection of Jesus only after they have undertaken a critique of the modern secular imagination that has influenced their orientation toward reality. Those who have come under the influence of the modern secular imagination and its sustaining ideologies, however subtle this influence has been, can redeem their own imaginations from the prejudices of the modern imagination by understanding its genealogy. This understanding occurs as a result of the evaluative criticism of rationalism, scientism, naturalism, materialism, atheism, and nihilism. The evaluative criticism of the modern secular imagination and its sustaining ideologies has already begun in society at large but has not as yet fully bloomed. This critique of the modern imagination will come from a postmodern vantage point.

The Postmodern Critique

The term postmodern has been used in scholarly writing since the 1950's and 1960's. At the time of this writing (1996) the word is used frequently in scholarly articles in a variety of professional fields. Postmodernism in architecture, literature, politics, mass communications, and philosophy has been discussed seriously at this point of its development.[39] It is beyond the scope of this book to engage in a lengthy analysis of postmodernism. A few comments, however, are necessary to relate the modern imagination to postmodern criticism.

First, the uses put to the notion of postmodernism are varied. It almost seems that the use of the word has become a fad. When nearly everything is said to be postmodern, the term begins to signify nothing. If postmodernism is the governing paradigm of our times, the paradigm is nearly impossible to define precisely. This is because the contemporary intellectual world of any time period is opaque and difficult to understand unless in retrospect. The governing paradigm of our time, I submit, cannot be elaborated exhaustively until it begins to pass away.

Second, in the absence of a generally-shared consensus about the meaning of postmodernism in philosophical and theological discourse, it is necessary for those who employ the term to stipulate its meaning. To do this, it is necessary also to define modernism.

Thomas C. Oden defines modernism as it is referenced to theology in terms of three distinct strata of meanings or three concentric circles of a bull's-eye. The outermost circle relates to modernity in the sense of "the overarching intellectual ideology of a historical period whose hegemony has lasted from the French revolution to the present...The second intermediate circle...defines modernity as a mentality, found especially among certain intellectual elites, which assumes that chronologically recent ways of knowing the truth are self-evidently superior to all premodern alternatives...The inner circle...is modernity in the sense of a later-stage deterioration of both of the preceding viewpoints."[40] Oden's definitions are helpful in establishing modernism as something that is to be transcended in postmodernism.

In another sense, modernism is a rage for what is current, up-to-date, and new. This rage, and I use the word purposely to suggest a perfervent passion for what is in fashion, was one of the bases of the French Revolution and for many philosophical trends that were initiated during the European Enlightenment. Simon Schama, in *Citizens: A Chronicle of the French Revolution,* maintains that the ruling elite from the king downward, including the so-called *philosophes* such as Voltaire, Diderot, Condillac, d'Alembert, Helvetius, d'Holbach, Condorcet, and others were less obsessed with the tradition they hated than with novelty in itself. Detestation of tradition did not promote revolutionary excesses as much as an infatuation with change, novelty, and the fixation on the latest fad, intellectual or otherwise.[41]

For me the concept of postmodernism refers to a *vantage point* in time and culture that gives perspective and grants discernment of the ideological currents of the previous three centuries. The concept also implies a *critique* of modernism and a critical assessment of the main currents of thought that dominated the Enlightenment period down to the present time. Finally, the idea of postmodernism in architecture suggested a harkening back to forms and styles prior to the modern period. In my use of the term postmodernism, a *retrieval* of certain pre-Enlightenment ideals and concepts is definitely implied. This does not mean, however, that I wish to call premodernism, whole and entire, back from exile to take the throne. There are elements of premodernism and classical periods, however, that deserve a second look.

David Tracy presents an interesting description of the classic. "If, even once, a person has experienced a text, a gesture, an image, and event, a person with the force of the recognition: 'This is important! This does make and will make a difference!' then one has experienced a candidate for classic status."[42] Certainly such texts, images, events, and persons have existed prior to the modern period, and demand retrieval and reflection.

Viewpoint and Discernment. We may not be able presently, as I observed above, to ascertain the precise nature of postmodernism since it is next to impossible to gain a complete view of "the contemporary" on a contemporaneous basis. Any period's governing paradigm can be examined closely in retrospect and after the paradigm has developed fully. Hindsight is always privileged. It is by means of critical hindsight that we are able to understand the modern secular imagination to an extent not possible in earlier times. We know there has been a shift of paradigmatic modern secular imagination because we "see" or understand the modern secular imagination as never before.

We are able today to look more astutely at the ideologies that have dominated the past three centuries because these ideologies came into full flower. We are able to gain a more insightful understanding of these ideologies because we can observe them not only as abstract systems but as "performances" as they play themselves out in the everyday world. We can take account of the "track records" of modern ideologies and conclude fairly that they are wanting. Much of the substance of modern ideologies is based on the anti-tradition prejudices of the Enlightenment, the absolutization of human reason, and the fantasy that anyone can address disputed issues completely free of biases and presuppostions, i.e., that anyone can look at things from a purely objective point of view and eventually gain knowledge utouched by prejudices.

We are able to evaluate more dispassionately today, and more critically than ever before, the programs of the ideologies responsible for the modern secular imagination. We now understand that there are no mathematical methods for securing perfect and objective knowlege. We understand that the search after knowledge untainted by human subjectivity is a fool's errand. The very act of knowing is the act of a knowing *subject*. We understand that human reason has its limitations and that there are alternative models of rationality, that science at any given time is guided by the suppositions of given paradigms, that naturalism is not a matter of rigorous inference as much as it is a judgment based on the predispositions of certain individuals, that materialism and atheism are not the conclusions of a rigorous scientific process but the suppositions of particular scientists. Harold Brown writes "we must diassociate ourselves from the view that objectivity requires that we approach our subject without preconceptions. As has been regularly pointed out by philosophers, sociologists, linguists, anthropologists, historians, and others, we cannot approach any subject matter in this state, and if we could, we would not know what questions to ask, and what answers to accept."[43]

Hans-Georg Gadamer observes that prejudices—provisional judgments imposed by one's tradition to enable responses to events in certain ways—forestructure understanding and incline individuals to interpret things from the vantage point sanctioned by his or her tradition in accord with the values of the tradition. "Prejudices are not necessarily unjustified and erroneous, so that they inevitably distort the truth. In fact, the historicity of our existence entails that prejudices in the literal sense of the word, constitute the initial directedness of our whole ability to experience."[44] A perfectly open mind is possible only for someone who has not profited from any experience. On the basis of the intellectual traditions that shape their outlooks, people prefer some answers to others; they prefer some questions to others. (This is not to say that prejudices need not be examined. Prejudices should be checked and evaluated. If any preliminary judgments are found wanting, they should be changed).

The fruit of the postmodern critique, to state the matter simply, is that a new day has dawned. The light of this new day has shown us that the ideals of the modern secular imagination are unattainable. We cannot secure a perfectly objective view of the world because we are caught up in the very workings of the world. Human reason has finally arrived on the scene to tell us that human reason is not perfect. Naturalism is not so much an inference based on evidence and drawn by means of critical thinking as it is a mere presupposition or even a hope of those who are radically opposed to religion. It is frivolous to make science into a new religion. The paradigms that guide scientific discovery themselves change and bring new ways of thinking.

Materialism today, particularly when matter itself presents itself as a mystery, belongs to a more primitive intellectual period. Atheism (and Deism) are often pragmatic postulates of revolutionary movements that promise to raise humans from inhumane conditions to a new dignity.[45] Atheism is based on the assumption that in killing God (the King), men and women will be free. All this we can see in the postmodern critique, and more.

New Insights into "The Possible."

There was a time when men and women began their reflections on the big questions of life in awe or wonder. Who has not been caught up in this awe while gazing into the immensity of a starry country sky? Plato taught that "the sense of wonder is the mark of the philosopher. Philosophy indeed has no other origin, and he was a good genealogist who made Iris the daughter of Thaumas."[46] That is, Iris is the goddess of the rainbow and a messenger of the gods; Thaumas is the prompter of wonder. With wonder intact and active, the human imagination is not artificially limited; the human imagination opens itself invitingly to reality however extraordinary reality may be.

Wonder, however, was replaced by Descartes as the starting point of philosophy, as the initial effort exerted by a "lover of wisdom." Philosophy, according to Descartes, begins in doubt. "Just as when Descartes set up an artificial and hyperbolical doubt, like an experiment, in his famous meditation on doubt, so methodological science fundamentally doubts everything that can be doubted," writes Gadamer, "in order to achieve in this way the certainty of its results." Doubt, as a primary ambience of reflection and research, often turns into suspicion and even skepticism in the modern imagination. The passion for certainty in the modern imagination, in turn, frequently becomes a neurotic obsession. The heralding of Jesus' resurrection easily can become a matter that is quickly dismissed when someone neglects an interrogation of the modern imagination as to its roots and causes.

Things have changed, however. From a perspective in the latter part of the 20th century that we call the postmodern perspective, we are able to see all of the marvels wrought by modern science, technology, and engineering. Many of these marvels have been put to destructive use; many others have benefited humanity in ways that challenge the imagination. Some of the wonders wrought by modern science, technology, and engineering have even transformed the modern secular imagination and enabled it to grasp that what was thought impossible prior to the age of invention is, indeed, possible.

A few years ago I visited the grave of a great grandmother in Iowa. Her name was Susan Coyle. She was born in County Down, Ireland, in 1820. During my reveries at her grave site, I wondered at the differences in the two worlds we respectively inhabited. Suppose, I wondered, that I could have somehow visited with her when she came to America at the height of the potato famine in the 1840's. Suppose I told her about my world.

In my world, I would have told her, I have flown from Boston to Shannon, Ireland, in five hours in an enclosed "ship" that carried over 350 persons. The ship flew nearly seven miles above the earth at 500 miles per hour. When I arrived in Ireland, I talked to my sister in America by means of a telephone. The telephone signals that carried our voices were bounced off a satellite that had been placed in the sky by men and women who flew over a hundred miles above the earth in earth orbit. Some men, of course, had walked on the surface of the moon relatively early in the exploration of our planetary system. Later in the same day that I had flown across the Atlantic, I would have told my great grandmother, I turned down the electric lights in my room and watched a soccer game on what we call television. The game was received in Ireland from Germany. What would have been my great grandmother's reaction? If she loved me and trusted me and possessed a large enough imagination, she would probably have believed me against everything her experience told her. She would have had a great difficulty imagining what I told her, but at least she would probably try. Love does such things.

Never mind about the capacity of imagination of persons who lived in the 1840's! Those of us who remember when, in our youth, ice wagons and milk wagons were pulled by horses in the city streets, are staggered when we review what has been accomplished in our lifetimes: jet airplanes, television, open-heart surgery, computers, DNA mapping, refrigerators, tape recorders, laser printers, laser surgery, microwave ovens, micro-chip technology, calculators, heart-lung machines, kidney dialysis machines, organ transplants, electron microscopes, nuclear energy generation, compact disks, and many more innovations that have visited us in the space of one lifetime. Increasingly as we grew older, the impossible became more probable. Our imaginations were stretched. The paradigms that governed the imaginations we used in interpretive analysis took on a new character. Our ideas of what was possible changed and broadened. We were awed by what human beings brought forth out of possibility into reality. Perhaps we began to realize experientially and not merely know abstractly that with God all things are possible, and that even the bodily resurrection of Jesus could be real in a sense we were never ready to imagine.

While the modern secular imagination in all of its various ideological strands pronounced the resurrection of Jesus impossible, the innovations brought about by the modern technological imagination, on the contrary, spoke out and declared that one must not place capricious limits on what is possible. While the modern secular imagination clashed with the paradigmatic Christian imagination in some ways, the modern secular imagination itself took on greater breadth and acquired—in the light of human innovations—a new respect for the immense range of what is possible. The Christian imagination was severely constricted by modern ideologies while at the same time, paradoxically, it was liberated from a confining narrowness due to the innovations of modern science and technology.

We may very well be presently located at the frontiers of the post-modern imagination. The postmodern imagination is as wide, broad, and vast as the science fiction it produces. The postmodern imagination is not quick to pronounce arbitrary limits on what is possible. The postmodern imagination can be supportive of the Christian image of the resurrection of Jesus and, if not supportive, at least open to the possibility of the resurrection. In this, the postmodern imagination is not naive or unsophisticated. On the contrary, it is astutely receptive in a new way of looking at traditional images of what is possible, images that are not foreign to the Christian paradigmatic imagination.

Concluding Remarks

We believe only what we deem possible. If our minds cannot grasp that a particular belief is within the realm of what is possible, the belief will find few, if any, who will accept it. When an image runs counter to what we imagine as constituing reality, that image either becomes classed under the category of fiction or is discarded as unreal.

The modern secular imagination, supported by the ideologies that grew of the Enlightenment, is not large enough to contain images of anyone who is raised from the dead, even if this resurrection occurs by the hand of God. Atheism (or its more socially acceptable and faddish cousins Deism, agnosticism, and nihilism) is the eventual trump card that must be played by those who argue forcefully against the possibility of the resurrection. Militant opponents of the image of the resurrection are fully aware that "for God all things are possible"(Mt 19:26). It is necessary, for those who deny the possibility of Jesus' resurrection, to deny the God who is the Lord of the Possible.

Paradoxically, while the Enlightenment was the soil out of which grew the ideologies that limited the human imagination, the science and technology fostered by the Enlightenment gives us cause today to stretch the human imagination. We see before us, and even use on a daily basis, technologies that would never have been viewed as possible 150 years ago. Likewise, with the advent of the postmodern period—a time wherein the assumptions of absolute certainty and objectivity are seen as fictions—we understand as never before that the sustaining ideologies of the modern imagination are liable to withering criticism. The bonds that would hold

Notes to Chapter 4

1. A careful distinction between pluralism and relativism is necessary lest we become stuck in the morass of relativism that maintains all points of view are equivalent. I would argue that within a plurality of interpretations about any issue, none is perfectly correct due to the limitations of language. All interpretations fall short of presenting the world as it actually is. Some interpretations, however, are less "distanced" from the truth than others. Some matters are so complex they cannot be expressed with absolute clarity. For an excellent treatment of this topic see Jeff Astley's chapter "Relativism, Religion, and Education" in his book *The Philosophy of Christian Religious Education* (Birmingham, AL: Religious Education Press, 1994), 257–289.
2. A.R. Manser, "Imagination," ed. Paul Edwards, *The Encyclopedia of Philosophy* (New York: Collier Macmillan, 1972), 4, 136–138.
3. Mary Warnock, *Imagination* (Berkeley, CA: University of California Press, 1976), 194.
4. Ibid., 196.
5. Ibid., 196.
6. Edward A. Casey, *Imagining: A Phenomenological Study* (Bloomington, IN: Indiana University Press, Midland Book, 1979), 138–139.
7. Garrett Green, *Imagining God: Theology and the Religious Imagination* (San Francisco: Harper and Row, 1989, p.73. I have borrowed the concept of the paradigmatic imagination from Garrett Green. He should not be held accountable for my reflections on, and characterizations of, the paradigmatic imagination.
8. Dennis Nineham, quoted in "Religious Imagination" by Mary Warnock, ed. James Mackey, *Religious Imagination* (Edinburgh: Edinburgh University Press, 1986), 156.
9. Mary Warnock, "Religious Imagination," 147.
10. The Enlightenment period of intellectual history as it is used here refers to the intellectual ferment that took place, principally in Europe, during the previous 300 years. During the Enlightenment, human progress was viewed as linked to radical individualism, rationality of judgment, the progress of empirical science, and an intolerance for traditionality. See Edward Shils' *Tradition* (Chicago: University of Chicago Press, 1981), 4–11.
11. The ideologies or "isms" were not produced *necessarily* by Enlightenment think-

ing. Narrow rationalism is a miscontrual of rationality, an excessive emphasis on reason. Scientism is a miscomprehension of science, the elevation of empirical knowledge over all other forms of understanding. Naturalism rejects *a priori* any reality transcendent to the world of our immediate experience, Materialism reduces all of reality to matter, a concept that is itself questioned by some contemporary scientists. Atheism either rejects God to raise up humankind, e.g., Auguste Comte's Positivism, or fails to grasp that religious thinkers have maintained that God is ultimately ineffable. Agnosticism limits knowledge to empirical knowledge and then claims God cannot be known. Agnosticism is an epistemological doctrine long before it has anything to do with God. Religious thinkers would not deny empirical knowledge is important; they refuse, however, to set arbitrary limits on the meaning of knowledge. Nihilism of the variety promoted by Nietszche rejects religious values for the purpose of creating a new kind of Superhuman. This new Superhuman bows down to no one, not even to God.

12. Philip Davis and Reuben Hersh, *Descartes' Dream: The World According to Mathematics* (Boston: Houghton Mifflin Co., 1986), 3–5.
13. William Barrett, *Death of the Soul: From Descartes to the Computer* (Garden City, NY: Anchor Books, 1987), xv.
14. Carl Sagan, *Broca's Brain* (New York: Random House, 1979), 282–283.
15. Ibid., 285.
16. Ibid., 286.
17. Andrew White, *A History of the Warfare of Science with Theology in Christendom* (Buffalo, NY: Prometheus Books, 1993), 2, 394. Herbert Spencer was a 19th century British philosopher, an agnostic, who applied the idea of evolution to all branches of knowledge.
18. Charles Darwin, *The Origin of the Species and the Descent of Man* (New York: Modern Library, nd), p. 64.
19. Ibid., 64.
20. Phillip E. Johnson, "Evolution as Dogma: The Establishment of Naturalism," *First Things,* 6, 1990, 19.
21. George Santayana, *Atoms of Thought* (New York: Philosophical Library, 1950), 234.
22. Ibid., 242.
23. Ibid., 55–56.
24. John Dewey, "What I Believe," in *John Dewey: The Later Works, 1925–1953* (Carbondale, IL: Southern Illinois University Press, 1984), 5, 267.
25. Ibid., 268.
26. Ibid., 269.
27. There are many kinds of humanism and even Christian humanism. Secular humanism is ordinarily opposed to any kind of religious humanism. In this, it is sometimes called Promethean humanism, a humanism that defies God because God, in the words Dietrich Kerler, "would set limits to my greatness." Quoted in Henri de Lubac's *The Drama of Atheist Humanism* (New York: New American Library, Meridian Book, 1963), 27.
28. Corliss Lamont, *The Philosophy of Humanism* (New York: Philosophical Library,

1957), 10.

29. Ibid., 18.

30. Charles Mayer, *Man: Mind or Matter?* (Boston: Beacon Press, 1951), 4–6.

31. Karl Marx, *Karl Marx: Essential Writings,* ed. Frederic Bender, trans. R. Dixon (New York: Harper and Row, Publishers, 1972), 144–151.

32. See William L. McBride, *The Philosophy of Marx* (New York: St. Martin's Press, 1977), 79–91.

33. Sigmund Freud, *The Standard Edition of the Complete Works of Sigmund Freud,* trans. and ed. James Strachey, from *Moses and Monotheism* (London: The Hogarth Press, 1981), 23, 55.

34. Sigmund Freud, *The Standard Edition of the Complete Works of Sigmund Freud,* trans. and ed. James Strachey, from *The Future of an Illusion* (London: The Hogarth Press, 1981), 21, 19.

35 Ibid., 39.

36. Francis Crick, *The Astonishing Hypothesis: The Scientific Search for the Soul* (New York: Charles Scribner's Sons, 1994), 6.

37. Ibid., 7.

38. Friedrich Nietzsche, *The Gay Science*, trans. Walter Kaufman (New York: Random House, 1974), p. 181.

39. See Steven Connor, *Postmodernist Culture: An Introduction to Theories of the Contemporary* (Cambridge, MA: Basil Blackwell Inc), 1991.

40. Thomas C. Oden, *After Modernity...What? Agenda for Theology* (Grand Rapids, Zondervan Publishing House, 1990), 46.

41. Simon Schama, *Citizens: A Chronicle of the French Revolution* (New York: Alfred A. Knopf, 1989).

42. David Tracy, *The Analogical Imagination: Christian Theology and the Culture of Pluralism* New York: Crossroad Publishing Company, 1996), 115–116.

43. Harold Brown, *Rationality* (New York: Routledge, 1990), 203.

44. Hans-Georg Gadamer, *Philosophical Hermeneutics,* trans. David Lange (Berkeley: University of California Press, 1977), 9.

45. The physicist John Barrow presents an illuminating portrait of "schizophrenic matter" in which he discusses the unexpected nature of microscopic particles of matter. See his book *The World within the World* (Oxford: Oxford University Press, 1990), 132–137. Also, see the physicist Paul Davies' discussion of the atom in *The Mind of God: The Scientific Basis for a Rational World* (New York: Simon & Schuster Touchstone Book, 1992), 85.

46. Plato, "Thaetetus," *The Collected Works of Plato,* trans. F. M. Cornford, eds. Edith Hamilton & Huntington Cairns, (Princeton: Princeton University Press, 1973), 860.

47. Hans-Georg Gadamer, *Truth and Method,* trans. J.C.B. Mohr (New York: Crossroad

5

THE RISEN CHRIST TODAY

Four paramount issues are examined in this concluding chapter. The first question refers to the manner in which contemporary Biblical scholarship interprets the resurrection of Jesus. The resurrection is viewed by reputable Christian scholars as an event that is unique and mysteriously singular in the story of humankind. A brief survey of contemporary scholarly understandings of the resurrection introduces the theme of this chapter.

The second point concerns the manner in which the risen Jesus is encountered today. Jesus arose into the glory of his Father, but that was not the end of his presence upon the earth. Jesus arose into three primary modes of presence in the world: 1) a presence in his Church, 2) a Biblical presence in the reading of the Word of God and 3) a Sacramental presence in the Eucharist, the bread and cup of the Lord's Supper. In these primary but not exclusive modes of presence, the risen Jesus is encountered today as a summons. This summons invites the response of faith.

The ability to see one thing as another, as noted in the previous chapter, is the function of the religious imagination. It is proposed that the risen Lord be interpreted as Church, Word, and Sacrament not in any "merely" symbolic way but as a real presence. The notion of real presence is explicated below in a manner, I hope, most Christians will be able to accept intellectually if not dispositionally.

The third issue of the chapter may be framed in a question: How are people able to respond affirmatively to the risen Jesus despite the dominant influence of the modern secular imagination, a naturalistic imagination that is often hostile to religion? It is suggested that those who encounter the presence of Jesus in Church, Word, and/or Sacrament "see through" the surface of things on the basis of religious faith.

Remember, according to Mary Warnock, the religious imagination enables individuals to "see through" the veneer of reality to its meaning.[1] The religious imagination empowers people with an insight that goes beyond a mere sighting of the world. Believers experience the risen Lord who is simultaneously concealed and revealed in Church, Word, and Sacrament. He is concealed in modes of presence that mediate his presence: the all too human faces of the members of his mystical body, the Church, in an always ambiguous human language in the Bible, and in the material elements of bread and wine in the Eucharist. He is revealed in what he accomplishes in the world as present in Church, Word, and Sacrament. The Christian imagination allows the believer to get beyond the concealments associated with the *modes* of Jesus' presence to his *presence* itself. The experience of the risen Jesus results as a consequence of their acceptance of the natural dispositions generated by the resurrection archetype, a loving and trusting faith, and the power of the Spirit of Christ.

It could be argued, of course, that the claims made here—that the risen Jesus is met in Church, Word, and Sacrament—simply avoids the entire issue of the resurrection as an apologetical problem. The fourth principal matter investigated, therefore, is the problematic nature of the resurrection, i.e., is the resurrection of Jesus primarily or exclusively an intellectual/apologetical concern or is it an existential/spiritual question? An intellectual problem may be debated in terms of discursive logic on the grounds of empirical evidence. An existential/spiritual problem, on the other hand, is one that confronts individuals in respect to certain questions: What should I believe? What may I hope? How should I comport myself in the workaday world? To what extent can I remain open to the possibility of Jesus' presence in the contemporary world? What stance must I take when I begin to "see through" things to the presence of the risen Lord? What should be my most important commitments?.

Introduction: The Resurrection in Contemporary Scholarship

E. P. Sanders offers a critical reflection on the resurrection. In this reflection he observes that those who offered testimony regarding the reality of the risen Jesus were clear about the extraordinary character of Jesus' manifestation to them. The risen Jesus was not a ghost, a resuscitated corpse, or a badly wounded man. His appearance was such that it beggared existing categories of their experience. Jesus was recognized in his "spiritual body," a compound concept most difficult to understand by those who learned that "spirit" and "body" were conflicting ideas. Sanders indicates he recognizes as factual that Jesus' followers and Paul had resurrection experiences. "What the reality was that gave rise to the experiences," Sanders writes, " I do not know...Nothing is more mysterious than the stories of (Jesus') resurrection, which attempt to portray an experience that the authors could not themselves comprehend."[2]

Why did the witnesses to the resurrection find it impossible to comprehend their experiences of the risen Jesus? The resurrection of Jesus, I suggest, is the only credible resurrection from the dead in history and as such is unique in the fullest sense of the word. Since the resurrection is a singular event of its kind, the resurrection experiences of Jesus' followers exhaust classification schemas available for sorting out historical events. Now, all historical events are unique, but in a sense different from the unique singularity of Jesus' resurrection. In themselves ordinary historical events occur only once; these events, however, can be fitted into a class of similar events. The resurrection of Jesus, however, is a unique event that transcends all *classes* of unique events. For example, Mary is a unique individual, but Mary is a human being and falls into the class known as "human" and into the class known as "woman." The resurrection event is unique and is unclassifiable according to our notional and linguistic categories.

The resurrection does not fit into ordinary categories of human history or experience. Neither can the resurrection be discussed adequately because it transcends customary language. When something is radically distinctive, it surpasses the possibility of being interpreted adequately, it remains a mystery. It is not as if we have multiple credible resurrections that allow us to draw up a categorization of Jesus' resurrection based on genus, species, and specific difference. Those who experienced the risen Jesus had nothing against which they could measure, classify, or assess their experiences.While the resurrection may be considered historical from one perspective, since it was an event within the temporal process, from another point of view the resurrection may not be judged to be historical. Historical events are classified into categories and compared with other historical events. This enables individuals to make interpretive judgments about the events. The apostles lacked the ability to classify and compare the resurrection event with other resurrections because there were no other resurrections. Not only were they unable to understand the resurrection clearly due to the singularity of the occurrence, but they were unable to state how the resurrection of Jesus was similar to, and distinct from, other historical resurrections.

This confusion over "naming" the precise nature of their experiences of the resurrection, it should be added, led eventually to divergent and conflicting narratives of Jesus' resurrection. The fact that all of the New Testament accounts of the resurrection do not agree in every aspect is often used by those who argue against the actuality of the resurrection. Quite another conclusion seems more congruent with the evidence. Various individuals and groups experienced the risen Jesus as a mysteriously singular event that transcended their abilities to "name" the event. Given this fact, it is far more reasonable to expect their separate accounts of the risen Jesus would conflict in many ways just as the accounts of witnesses of traffic accidents often differ in many ways. The experience of any exceptional event by several people *ordinarily* leads to narratives of the event that are at odds with one another. The differences among the resurrection narratives point not to the deception of the witnesses but instead to the authenticity of the narratives as accounts of a mysteriously singular historic event, an historical event so different from other historical events that it is possible for some to interpret the event as non-historical. The question, "What is historical knowledge?" comes to the fore. Can an event that is radically unique and incomparable, since there are no similar events, be called historical? The matter is essentially a definitional problem vis-a-vis the concept of historical knowledge.

Another contemporary scholar, John P. Meier, writes that a treatment of the resurrection is omitted from his acclaimed two-volume work *A Marginal Jew: Rethinking the Historical Jesus*. The resurrection is not discussed "not because it is denied but simply because the restrictive definition of the historical Jesus I will be using does not allow us to proceed into matter that can be affirmed only by faith."[3]

If one defines historical analysis in terms of those events that were generally open and classifiable to anyone who happened to be in the vicinity where those events occurred, perhaps the resurrection of Jesus cannot be included as an historical event. Jesus appeared to those whose faith and openness were energized by the love they had for Jesus. Evidence in the New Testament seems to indicate that the blind were healed by Jesus when they believed in him. In Matthew 9:27-30, for example, Jesus said to the two blind men, "According to your faith let it (healing) be done to you. And their eyes were opened." The healing of physical blindness in this instance certainly is an analogue for the healing of spiritual blindness. Some things cannot be experienced without the trustful openness that comes from faith. Only faith makes some experiences accessible. Perhaps the resurrection appearances of Jesus were historical events for some (for those who possessed at least the beginnings of faith) and not for others (for those who would never believe even if someone risen from the dead would appear to them). On the other hand, it could very well have happened that the risen Jesus could have been seen by anyone. Whatever speculation we make about this event begins and ends in mystery, something one would expect about God's decisive word-event in human history.

What is underscored by Meier is the idea that historical events as defined by many of the most reputable Biblical scholars today extend only to those events that are accessible to all who would have been in proximate relationships to the events and from whom no special faith capacity is required. Further, Meier also stresses what I have referred to as the mysterious singularity of the resurrection. Again, as one reflects more and more on the question of Jesus' resurrection as an historical event, it seems one moves from the issue of the resurrection properly to an issue of language and definition.

In the preface to his two-volume work *The Death of the Messiah: From Gethsemane to the Grave*, Raymond E. Brown notes he was asked "by a surprising number of people" if intended to write a book on the resurrection of the Messiah. Prior to the book on the death of Jesus, Brown had also completed a book on the birth of the Messiah. A volume on the resurrection, in the minds of many, would complete a trilogy of scholarly tomes about Jesus. "Responding with mock indignation that I have written two books on the resurrection..., I tell them emphatically that I have no such plans. I would rather explore that area "face to face."[4]

Quite obviously Brown believes in the resurrection of Jesus. There is something enigmatic, however, about his comment that he had already written two books on the resurrection. What this scholar seems to be saying is that everything written about Jesus in the New Testament, from his birth to his sayings and deeds, and thence to his death would not have been written at all were it not for the resurrection faith of his followers. New Testament writings and the living witness of the Church are, after all, primary and direct consequences of belief in the resurrection of Jesus. Jesus died, was buried, was raised from the dead as the first-born from the dead (Col. 1:18) and, having been raised from the dead, Jesus is the first fruits of those who have died (1 Cor 15:20). Because Jesus was apprised as the first fruits of those who have died, the memory of Jesus moved his followers to shake the foundations of the world.

Juan Luis Segundo makes this point when he states that no matter "how we characterize the *datum* of Jesus' resurrection (as truth or illusion, objective experience or subjective mistake), we can scientifically prove with the documents at hand that the *experiences* constitutive of that *datum* were historically decisive for interpreting Jesus and thereby defining the meaning, function, and structure of the early Christian church."[5] The *experience* of the resurrected Jesus was possible perhaps only by those whose spiritual eyes were opened. The *consequences* of the experience are attested by historical evidences that may be examined by all.

In addition to locating the experiences of the risen Jesus outside of the definitions of the term "historical", and the appearances of the risen Jesus as confirming the already-existing faith of the witnesses, the question is raised by scholars as to where Jesus was thought to be present after his resurrection. Marinus de Jonge observes that once the followers of Jesus reflected on the resurrection, exaltation, and ascension of Jesus into heaven, they would have viewed the literature of the Hebrew Testament as referring, in a spiritual sense, to Jesus. Thus, Jesus' status after his death, resurrection, and exaltation would be seen in Psalm 110: 1. "The Lord says to my lord: 'Sit at my right hand, till I make your enemies your footstool." Jesus arose into the glory of God and sits at the right hand of his Father.[6] What is added to this, however, is the notion of Jesus' return. In Mark 14:62, Jesus responds to the high priest who asked him, at his trial, if he was the messiah. "Jesus said, 'I am; you will see the Son of Man seated at the right hand of the Power, and coming with the clouds of heaven."" Many more references, not mentioned here for the sake of brevity, confirm early Christian belief that the risen Jesus is with his Father and will come again, in the words of the Apostles' Creed, "to judge the living and the dead."

But in another sense, Jesus remained with his Church and, from another perspective, he remained *in* his Church. "The early (Christian) community," states Pheme Perkins, "felt itself to be in contact with the active presence of the risen Lord. Different traditions have given different forms of expression to that sense of presence."[7] Perkins goes on in her chapter "Resurrection as Jesus' Presence" to examine several of these traditions.

In the epilogue of his book *Jesus: A New Vision*, Marcus Borg indicates the story of the *historical* Jesus ends with his death, but the story of Jesus does not end there. The followers of Jesus proclaimed that Jesus triumphed over death. Jesus remained a living reality for his followers. Jesus appeared to his followers but we do not know the nature of these appearances. We do not know what was precisely involved in the dynamics of the resurrection. The resurrection of Jesus was not a resuscitation of a corpse. On the contrary, Jesus is described as entering a new mode of being. On historical grounds, according to Borg, there is little we can say. We do know, however, that "Jesus' followers continued to experience him as a living reality, and *in a new way*, namely as having the qualities of God. Now he could be known anywhere, and not just in a particular place; now he was the presence which abided with them."[8] This notion of *presence* plays a major part in my own understanding of the risen Jesus today.

The resurrected Jesus is present today specifically, but not exclusively, I propose, in Church, Word, and Sacrament. Discussion of this topic can begin in a variety of ways. One of the more promising starting places is St. Paul's first letter to the Corinthians.

The Presence of Jesus Today

Aside from being the earliest written testimony of the tradition of Jesus' resurrection, the first letter to the Corinthians contains rich references to the Lord's Supper or Eucharist and material relevant to the thrust of this chapter about baptized Christians as members of the body of Christ.

The First Letter to the Corinthians

Anyone's initial reading of Paul's first letter to the Corinthians may question the unity and coherence of the composition. The letter does not appear to hang together well. While the letter was sent to the Christian assembly about 55 A.D.—Paul had visited Corinth perhaps five years earlier—what has come down to us today may be parts of three or four letters that were redacted much later into their current form as 1 and 2 Corinthians. As the New Testament canon began to be established in, say, 80 to 90 A.D., it became necessary for the church at Corinth to sort out papyri sheets sent to the church by Paul and to reconstruct the letters as best as possible.[9] If the letters to the Corinthians do not always seem internally consistent as regards the positioning of ideas, the situation can be attributed to editing that occurred long after the letters were composed and sent to Corinth.

The Church at Corinth: Background Information

Corinth became a Roman colony in 4 B.C. At the time of Paul's first letter to the church at Corinth, many former Roman soldiers lived there. Additionally there were Greeks, people from Asia Minor, and Jews. The city supported many pagan temples. The temple of Aphrodite, the goddess of love, was prominent among many temples in the city. Sailors and merchants from the near-by ports of Lechaion and Cenchrae visited Corinth on a regular basis. It is not unlikely that Corinth resembled most Mediterranean ports at the time in its rowdiness and immorality. The multiplicity of pagan religions represented in Corinth no doubt precipitated many discussions about gods and rites.

Paul established the church at Corinth about 50 A.D. After his visit to Athens (Acts 18:1-7), he preached in the Jewish synagogue of Corinth. His ministry was perhaps aided by Aquila and Priscilla, Roman Jews who had been banished from Rome, along with other Jews, by the emperor Claudius. As may have been usual, an uproar took place when Paul preached. Jews who supported the old ways argued with Paul and brought legal proceedings against him. The proconsul Gallio ruled that he could not legally intervene because the issues involved in the dispute revolved solely around Jewish religious matters (Acts 18:12-17). After 18 months of residence at Corinth, Paul left for Ephesus. The work of Paul at Corinth was continued by the orator Apollos of Alexandria, a convert from Judaism. The apostle Peter may also have been in Corinth at one time (1 Cor 12).[10]

1 Corinthians

What did Paul's first letter to the Corinthians contain? It seems there were problems of factionalism in the Christian community. Some members of the community had made idols, figuratively speaking, of some Christians leaders and teachers. Groups were formed and the unity of the church was threatened. Jealousy and quarreling became problematic (1 Cor 1:4 - 4:21). Paul also addressed specific moral issues such as sexual immorality, lawsuits among believers, and apparently a lack of respect for the body. This may have been due to a reoccurring tendency in the early Church to disdain the body and magnify the importance of the soul. "The body is not meant for fornication," wrote Paul, "but for the Lord, and the Lord for the body. And God raised the Lord and will raise us by his power. Do you not know that your bodies are members of Christ?" (1 Cor

6:13-15). This theme is explored by Paul later in the letter.

In the next section of the letter Paul discusses Christian marriage and various problems that beset the Christian community (1 Cor 7:1-40). This is followed by directions for problems regarding the eating of meat sacrificed to idols, a brief discourse on the rights of an apostle, and an exhortation to maintain the faith under trying circumstances. "Do you not know in a race the runners all compete, but only one receives the prize? Run in such a way that you may win it."(1 Cor 9:24). The section concludes with an admonition against abuses at the Lord's Supper and the institution of the Eucharist, themes that are examined in greater detail below.

The next segment of the letter considers rules for liturgical celebrations, problems in the celebration of the Lord's Supper or Eucharist, and the teaching that there is only one Spirit of Christ and one body of the faithful despite the many diverse gifts of the Spirit that are given to the Church (1 Cor 11:2 - 14:40). Next, Paul explains the teaching of the resurrection of the body in (1 Cor 15: 1-58). In his exposition on the meaning of the resurrection Paul stresses that Jesus' resurrection would have been in vain if the members of Christ's body do not also rise from the dead. What the Corinthians were contesting primarily was not the resurrection of Jesus but their own future resurrection. No doubt there were those among the Corinthians whose disdain for the body was proportionate to their extreme glorification of the spirit. Finally, the letter is brought to a conclusion in the last chapter. Paul arranges for a collection for the church in Jerusalem, he tells the Corinthians of his plans for travel, and sends his final messages and greeting (1 Cor 16:1-22).

Encountering Jesus Today

Jesus may be encountered today, in a very real sense, in the modalities of presence in the Church, Biblical Word, and the Lord's Supper or Eucharist. He is encountered, furthermore, as someone who is really present in Church, Word, and Sacrament. That is, the presence of Jesus in the contemporary world is not a mere figurative presence. Jesus is authentically and genuinely present as risen Lord, for those who know how to see, i.e., for those whose Christian paradigmatic imagination is developed.

The Presence of Jesus in the Church

In the first letter to the Corinthians, in response to what Paul had heard about divisions in the church of Corinth, he reminds the Corinthians that they were baptized, in one Spirit, into one body. "For just as the body is one and has many members, and all the members of the body, though many, are one body, so it is with Christ. For in one Spirit we were all baptized into one body—Jews, Greeks, slaves or free—and were all made to drink of one Spirit." (1 Cor 12:12-13). Paul goes on to show that there are many functions of the body but all of the functions ultimately redound to the body considered as a whole. His beautiful and celebrated remarks on the gift of love follow his comments about the unity of the body. Love is what makes for unity.

More to point of this chapter is the teaching that Christ is in the world in the members of his mystical body. This concept is one of the primary images in Paul's consciousness (Rom 12:5; 1 Cor 12:13, 37; Eph 1:22-23, 4:4,12,16; Col 1:18, 2:17, 3:15). Paul "thought of the body of Christ as present, active, and purified for his manifestation to the world after he was no longer flesh. The body in which he is now present is the body of believers."[11]

In this teaching about the mystical body of Christ, Paul instructed the Corinthians, in other words, to interpret the Christian community imaginatively *as* the presence of Christ in the midst of the world. The question that follows upon this is crucial: Were the Corinthians to think of themselves as the body of Christ in some metaphorical sense or in a real sense? Was Paul indulging in mere allegorical writing or were his words to be construed in a manner that indicated the real presence of Jesus in the body of believers, the body animated by the Spirit of Christ? Did the Corinthians interpret Paul's teaching as suggesting they must simply pretend to be the body of Christ or as advising they were actually the new bodily manifestation of Christ in human history? Were Christians the extensions of Christ in the world in a moral sense as a group of Platonic philosophers might have been the extension of Plato in the world? The question is extremely important for Christians in regard to their religious identity.

Metaphor and Truth. The Eucharist is more than a *mere* symbol and less than the physical presence of Jesus in the form of a man. Much like a metaphor—something that is neither a truth in ordinary terms or a simple apparent lie—the Eucharist is simultaneously the presence of Jesus in a different mode of presence and the absence of Jesus in his physical form of a man. The Eucharist, it seems, is something like a visual metaphor. It is this concept of metaphor that attracts our present attention. The presence of the risen Jesus in the Eucharist is discussed more fully later in the chapter.

Earl Mac Cormac has noted that some theorists—controversionists by name—maintain metaphors assert false statements when taken literally, e.g., John's blood is boiling. In this example, of course, John's blood is not really boiling in the sense the molecules in his blood are excited by physical heat. This false statement about John, however, describes his temperament at a particular time in a dramatic, and perhaps not untruthful, way. From one point of view the statement is false; from another perspective the statement is true. Of course, if John is sufficiently exercised over some problem, his body temperature may rise considerably. One of the problems with controversionism is the ambiguity associated with the word literal.[12] If the literal meaning of any word is the meaning intended by the speaker or writer, and if the individual who says "John blood is boiling" intends that John is heating up emotionally, is the proposition about John really false?

Mac Cormac does not accept controversionist theory but avers "that all metaphors are true to a degree; that is, through their novel juxtapositions they express insights that are proper assertions."[13] He discusses epiphors, i.e., metaphors that *express* insights of which we were previously unaware until we are confronted with the metaphor as distinct from diaphors which *suggest* new meaning. In this discussion, Mac Cormac offers the following example of an epiphor: "Billboards are warts on the landscape." We detect immediately the similarity between ugly billboards and ugly warts on an otherwise smooth body. There is a truth in the epiphor and the expression itself is a new and dramatic way of declaring that truth. An epiphor is a *mode* of making meaning present in a novel and dramatic way. Is it mistaken to claim that Jesus' presence in Church, Bible, and Sacrament is an epiphoric presence, a presence that is not at all evident at the surfaces of reality but a presence nonetheless that can be recognized by those who know how to "see through" the surfaces of reality? Moreover, if truth can be really present and expressed in an epiphor, is it unthinkable to assess Church, Word, and Sacrament as visual epiphors?

Janet Martin Soskice writes that in regard to the interpretation of religious language, context must be taken into account. "The descriptive vocabulary which any individual uses is...dependent on the community of interest and investigation in which he finds himself, and the descriptive vocabulary which a community has at its disposal is embedded in particular traditions of investigation and conviction..."[14] For Christians this means that metaphors must be interpreted in relation to experience, community, and Christian interpretive tradition. Experience is the reference which grounds the interpretation, community provides a context for interpretation, and the interpretive tradition is what lends authority to the interpretation. The hermeneutical question, it seems, is as much one of language and tradition as it is a question of theology. Paul's teaching regarding Christians as members of the body of Christ, therefore, needs to be read interpretively in relation to the Christian community at Corinth, and in relation to the interpretive tradition of the church at Corinth. Since there is no exact and thorough knowledge today of the church at Corinth or its interpretive tradition, the best we can do is reconstruct the situation at Corinth to the best of our ability.

Members of the Christian community at Corinth would have recalled that they were baptized in the Spirit into one body of Christ (1 Cor 12:12). This baptism was not understood as a mere figurative initiation into a club or burial association but as something that radically transformed them, perhaps not psychologically (although this is likely) but instead ontologically. Their very *being* was transformed by baptism. "Do you not know that you are God's temple and that God's Spirit dwells in you?" Paul asks them in the letter (1 Cor 2:15). From all available evidence provided by the text of the first letter to the Corinthians and from the historical record of Acts, it would seem that Paul's reference to the incorporation of the baptized into the body of Christ was meant, on his part, to denote a real identification of Christ with those who received his Spirit in baptism. Further, this same evidence supports the claim that the Christians at Corinth, at Paul's instruction, would think of themselves as actual members of Christ, the Christ who was to continue the work of salvation through them.

"Baptism incorporates the Christian into the risen, glorified body of Christ, so that the Church, the assembly of the baptized, is the manifestation and extension of the Lord's body in this world," writes Richard Kugelman. "The Church is the body of Christ because it is composed of members who share in the life of the risen Lord."[15] Despite the limitations of its human administrative structures, the imperfections of its members, and the divisions within the Church, the risen Jesus is really present in his members today; it is here the risen Lord encounters those who do not identify with him today and summons them to faith and to the service of God's kingdom. It is here the risen Lord announces his presence, becomes a focus for the creation of community, serves those who are in need his help, and as the high priest of the New Covenant offers himself as a worthy sacrifice to his heavenly Father. Further, the risen Lord today in his Church teaches his people and bears witness to the world about his resurrection at the hand of his eternal Father.

The members of the Church are responsible for presenting Jesus to the world at large. They do this in the execution of various functions. Several technical terms have delineated these functions of the Church from New Testament times. We are accustomed to think of these functions in terms of what the followers of Jesus do in the world under the influence of the Holy Spirit. From another point of view, we can seen Jesus himself acting in the members of his Church carrying out ecclesial functions. The kerygmatic function (kerygma= message) occurs when the members of Christ's body proclaim Jesus as risen Lord. The koinoniac function (koinonia = community) concerns the participation of Christians in the fellowship of the Spirit of Christ. The diaconic function (diakonia = service) focuses on serving the corporal and spiritual needs of individuals whether they are members of the Church or those outside of the Church. The liturgical function (leitourgia = service in the sense of worship service) centers on the public worship of the Church. The didactic function (didache = teaching) is undertaken when the Church exercises its teaching through its members. Finally, the witness function (martyria = witness) of the Church consists in the public testimony of the Church that Jesus is Lord. Members of the body of Christ are instruments of his presence on earth. In another sense, it is the risen Jesus, active in those who are baptized into his death and resurrection, who is the one who encounters all the peoples of our planet in the functions outlined above.

All of these functions are important. The cardinal function, however, is perhaps the kerygmatic function, the heralding of the lordship of the risen Lord. All other functions, it seems to me, flow from the kerygma. The kerygma is implicitly present in all of the other works. It is in the performance of these functions that the Church invites people today to enter the kingdom of God. The Church as the instantiation of the risen Lord confronts individuals in the contemporary world and extends a summons to salvation. "The community of believers," observes Daniel Taylor, "is the 'context' within which most of us will 'recognize the Lord.'"[16]

If anyone is graced to experience the Church as the presence of Christ in history, a response of faith in Jesus as Lord is evoked. Each person's response of faith is invited in the initial meeting with the Church *as* Christ, an occurrence that is not always free of obscurity. Sometimes it is only in retrospect that one is aware of "meeting" the risen Lord in the Church. The individual's response of faith is sustained in the individual's ongoing relationship with the Church. Perhaps some Christians do not remember exactly when they first assented to the proclamation that Jesus is Lord. In many instances individuals "met" Jesus tacitly in the religious activities of their families, or in the events that took place in local churches or parishes. In this "meeting" they were summoned to faith tacitly and unobtrusively, and they said "yes" to the risen Lord in a general manner. The encounter with the risen Lord who is present in the members of his body is not ordinarily, initially, a formal matter at all.

The story of Malcolm Muggeridge's encounter with the risen Lord who is present in his Church is instructive. Muggeridge testifies that his deep dissatisfaction with prevailing contemporary values and assumptions led to his being possessed by an "abiding sense, ever more overwhelming in its intensity, that there is an alternative, an alternative that was first propounded two thousand years ago near the Sea of Galilee."[17] He goes on to write that the theological implications of his position were quite beyond him. What precipitated his conversion was an experience in Jerusalem in the midst of Christian pilgrims. "...seeing a party of Christian pilgrims at one of (the) shrines, their faces bright with faith, their voices, as they sang, so evidently and joyously aware of their Savior's nearness, I understood that for them the shrine was authentic. Their faith made it so. Similarly, I, too, became aware that there really had been a man, Jesus, who was also God: I was conscious of his presence."[18]

The response of faith may be purely notional for someone who considers an encounter with Jesus something of an intellectual exercise. The response of faith becomes more real when it engages all of a person's capacities, including the person's imagination. To someone who insisted on "proofs" of the resurrection of Jesus, I suggest that Jesus is "met" more genuinely in the midst of the members of his body than in labored arguments.

In the first chapter, I recounted meeting a stranger on the train who assured me that scholars had shown Jesus' resurrection to have been nothing but a revival myth in a long series of myths. I placed hardly any credence in his words. This was due, I believe, to the fact that I had met Jesus in his Church, and particularly those I knew in my parish community and those I loved in my family and circle of friends. Not all of the scholars from all of the great centers of learning around the world would have convinced me that Jesus was nothing but another mythical figure. Having "met" Jesus in his Church, other "proofs" were superfluous.

The Presence of Jesus in the Biblical Word

The Bible is the normative written account of God's saving deeds in human history. At the center of this account stands Jesus as the greatest of God's deeds. Both the Bible and the Lord's Supper or Eucharist can be understood only in reference to the Church. It was the Church that approved the canon of the Bible, both the Old and New Testaments, and it is within the public worship of the Church that the Bible is celebrated foremost as the Word of God. Indeed, the Bible is situated at the very heart of Christian public worship and the private religious devotions of Christians. The Bible is the foundation of Christian preaching and teaching. The Bible, in foreshadowing the coming of Jesus, in depicting the sayings and deeds of Jesus, and in pointing in hope to his return makes Jesus present today. All Scripture is referable to Jesus—directly or indirectly, immediately or remotely—and makes him present to the religious interpretive imagination.

The Biblical Word of God reaches its fullest power when it is communicated orally and not simply read silently. According to Raymond E. Brown, despite the fact the gospels were written works, "most Christians probably heard them... Hearing the gospels read publicly rather than reading them personally and privately was, arguably, the majority situation throughout most of Christian history."[19]

Walter J. Ong, writing about the expression "Word of God" in Hebrew and Greek tradition, notes several meanings that attach to the phrase. 1) the word of God signifies the exercise of God's power, e.g., God created the world with his word, 2) God's word is often understood as any communication from God to humanity, 3) the phrase may refer to God's communication to the prophets who speak out for him, 4) the expression can mean God's communication to the inspired writers of the Bible, 5) the word of God can also mean what is actually written in the original Biblical texts, and 6) there is the Word of God who is Jesus Christ.[20]

In Ong's view, the power of the word of God is exemplified in the spoken word. When God *utters* his word, the world is created; from all eternity God's *utterance* of his substantial Word is a person of the Trinity. "In the beginning was the Word and the Word was with God. He was in the beginning with God" (John 1:1-2). It is in the spoken word that the word itself leaves the "silence of the page" and becomes diffused broadly in the world. "The centrality of the spoken word as a point of reference for the various senses of the word of God is due not only to the fact that the spoken word is always primary (writing and print always refer directly or remotely to the world of sound) but also to the fact that the Bible... registers the oral culture still so dominant when the Bible came into being."[21] Even after the word of God had been reproduced in written form, the ancient practice was to read aloud. "Since the word itself was thus not anchored to the silence of the page with the exclusiveness which a typographical society would imagine necessary...the presence even of the written word was felt to be less confined to the surface of the page and to be more diffused through the whole of the social fabric than would be common after Gutenberg."[22]

The spoken word takes its power not only because it moves out into the world at large and is not confined to the page, but because it comes from the interior of the one who speaks the word. The word originates in the heart or in the interiority of the speaker thereby gaining the authority of the speaker. Another idea should be added here: In a typographical or visual culture, the watchword is "Seeing is believing." For Paul, however, "faith comes from what is heard..." (Rom: 10:17). In our present typographical society we strive for certainty, for clarity, and for perfect evidence before we believe. Evidently the apostle Thomas, at the report of Jesus's resurrection, was caught up in the wonders of the written word, at a time of transition between the old aural-oral culture and the new visual culture. "Unless I see the mark of the nails," Thomas vowed, "and put my finger in the mark of the nails and my hand in his side, I will not believe" (Jn 20:25). To believe on the word of others, however, a person must trust. Out of this trust, once it is practiced routinely within a collection of people, the collection becomes a community. Trust in the spoken word authenticated by a group of individuals leads to the acceptance of what is spoken and transforms that group of individuals into a community.

It is no wonder, then, that the written word of God attains its most powerful form when it is spoken aloud in liturgical services and when it is announced by preachers who explicate its relevance today. When teachers read and discuss the written word of God, this word gains ascendency over the hearts of those who hear it trustingly.

The Private Reading of Scripture. The foregoing emphasis on the vocal utterance of the Biblical Word should not stand against the private or devotional reading of the Bible. Jesus can also be "met" when an individual sits down and reads the Bible privately. One of the most famous instances of a conversion resulting from the private reading of the Bible is the case of St. Augustine of Hippo. Augustine struggled many years with the option of renouncing his sins and turning toward God. While his mother, known later as St. Monica, prayed for his conversion, Augustine listened to the preaching of someone who was also to be venerated as a saint, Ambrose, the bishop of Milan. One day Augustine asked himself how long he would postpone becoming a member of the Church. While he was "weeping in his heart" Augustine heard the voice of a child in a nearby house singing *"Tolle lege, tolle lege."* "Pick it up and read, pick it up and read," the voice commanded. Let Augustine complete the story in his own words:

> At this I looked up, thinking hard whether there was any kind of a game in which children used to chant words like these, but I could not remember... I stood up telling myself that this could only be a divine command to open my book of Scripture and read the first passage on which my eyes should fall. I seized the book (of Paul's epistles), opened it, and in silence I read the first passage on which my eyes fell: "(Let us pass our time honorably)...not in reveling and drunkenness, not in lust and wantonness, not in quarrels and rivalries. Rather, arm yourselves with the Lord Jesus Christ; spend no more thought on nature and nature's appetites" (Rom 13:13-14). I had no wish to read more and no need to do so. For in an instant as I came to the end of the sentence, it was as though the light of confidence flooded into my heart and all the darkness of doubt was dispelled."[23]

The private reading of the Bible can lead to the meeting of the risen Lord and quite often contributes not only to the activation of faith but also to the sustenance and growth of one's faith commitment and faith insight. The private reading of the Bible, then, is appropriately a potential meeting place where the risen Lord reveals himself to individuals notwithstanding the power of the Biblical Word when it is uttered publicly.

The Presence of Jesus in the Lord's Supper/Eucharist

It has already been observed that Paul corrected the Corinthians for their divisions and groups. This theme comes to the fore again in 1 Cor 11:17ff. Paul accuses them of coming together in separate cliques when they gather for the Lord's Supper. This furthers the divisions among them. "When you come together, it is not really to eat the Lord's Supper.

For when the time comes to eat, each of you goes ahead with your own supper, and one goes hungry and another becomes drunk" (1 Cor 11:20-21). One cannot help but wonder if class divisions came into play in the church at Corinth. Segregated eating arrangements according to social status was not uncommon among the Romans. Perhaps this practice was introduced when the Corinthian Christians came together for the Lord's Supper. Factionalism showed its deadly face again and this time it was at the common meal celebrated by the church, a meal that was no ordinary meal.

Paul uses the occasion to instruct the Corinthians on the meaning of the Lord's Supper. He does this by reciting the tradition that was handed on to him. The formulaic nature is almost obvious even in translation. "For I received from the Lord what I also handed on to you, that the Lord Jesus on the night when he was betrayed took a loaf of bread, and when he had given thanks, he broke it and said, 'This is my body that is for you. Do this in remembrance of me.' In the same way he took the cup also, after supper, saying , 'This cup is the new covenant in my blood. Do this, as often as you drink it, in remembrance of me.' For as often as you eat this bread and drink the cup, you proclaim the Lord's death until he comes" (1 Cor 11: 23-26). Paul continues to state that whoever eats the bread or drinks the cup of the Lord unworthily will be answerable for the body and blood of the Lord. "Examine yourselves, and only then eat of the bread and drink of the cup. For all who eat and drink without discerning the body, eat and drink judgment against themselves" (1 Cor 11: 28-29). Your entire purpose in the Lord's Supper, Paul argues, is to celebrate your oneness in Christ. You are one body in one Spirit and yet you behave as if you nothing more than a collection of cliques. Recognize what you are doing! Recognize what the Lord's Supper is all about! What is most astounding is that you do not recognize the Lord's presence among you in the Lord's Supper.

The eminent Scottish divine and New Testament scholar William Barclay claimed that there was no passage in the New Testament of greater interest that this. "For one thing, it gives us our warrant for the most sacred act of worship in the Church, the Sacrament of the Lord's Supper; and, for another since the letter to the Corinthians is earlier than the earliest of the gospels, this is actually the first recorded account we possess of any word of Jesus."[25]

The passage is important for another reason. Perhaps no passage in the New Testament has been interpreted in so many ways by Christians since, and even prior to, the Reformation. Barclay's approach to the passage is interesting. He distinguishes between interpreting the passage according to a crude literalism on the one hand, and empty symbolism on the other hand. Barclay states that since Jesus was still alive at the first Lord's Supper, the bread was easily distinguishable from his body. Therefore, he concludes, Jesus did not mean for his words to be taken literally. (We bump up against the mystifying word *literal* once again. For me the literal meaning of Jesus' words refers to the bread and wine of the Lord's Supper as another mode of presence. When Jesus said "This is my body" he meant "This is another mode of my presence with you until I come again."). Barclay continues by observing that the bread and wine of the Lord's Supper is more than a symbol. The words "This is my body" did not simply mean "This stands for my body." The broken bread of the Sacrament does stand for the body of Christ; but it does more, writes Barclay. "To him who takes it into his hands and upon his lips with faith and love, it is a means not only of memory but of living contact with Jesus Christ. To an unbeliever it would be nothing; to a lover of Christ it is the way to his presence."[26]

To affirm the Eucharist according to a crude literalism means, for me, to argue that the bread of the Lord's Supper is the physical equivalent of the body of Jesus. Thus, if one would put the bread under a microscope, one might expect to see human skin cells. This interpretation, I suggest, is not only crude but also frivolous.

To affirm the Eucharist according to a supposedly pure symbolism, on the other hand, is to miss the entire thrust of the ancient formula used in the Lord's Supper. The person who says that the Eucharist is a *mere* symbol debases the meaning of symbolism and assumes that all possible modes of divine presence are accounted for and known. There are empty symbols, I am sure, but there are also real symbols, symbols that are visual metaphors which express a truth or reality in a dramatic way. Until such a time as there is genuine ecumenical development leading to a widespread consensus among Christians vis-a-vis the presence of the risen Christ in the Eucharist, perhaps many of us will be forgiven for saying "I do not know how to explain it, but I believe Jesus is really present in the bread and cup of the Lord's Supper. I am able, thanks to my religious imagination, to see the appearances of bread and cup *as* the body and blood of the risen Lord. I am able to experience the Lord's Supper both *as* a celebration that points back to the sacrifice of Jesus on the cross and as a messianic banquet that points clearly ahead to the wedding feast we will celebrate in the heavenly meta-future, that Absolute Future beyond which there is no other."

In Luke's gospel (Lk 24:31) there is recounted the narrative of the two disciples who met Jesus on the road to Emmaus after the resurrection. Mark also makes brief mention of this (Mk 16: 12-13). The eyes of the disciples were unopened to the presence of Jesus until supper time. "When he was at table with them, he took bread, blessed and broke it, and gave it to them. Then their eyes were opened, and they recognized him; and he vanished from their sight." (Lk 24: 30-31). To paraphrase, the two disciples were unable to recognize the risen Jesus until he manifested himself to them in the bread of the Eucharist. The bread of the Eucharist, once unveiled by the Christian interpretive imagination, is experienced as the risen Lord. The Christian interpretive imagination, in turn, becomes operative only in the power of faith.

Christ Present in Church, Word, and Sacrament

Why did Jesus choose to be present in human history, after his ascension into heaven (Mk 16:19f; Lk 24:50ff; Acts 1:6ff), why did he elect to be present in his Church, in the Biblical Word, and in the Lord's Supper or Eucharist? There was probably little choice in the matter given the fact that community, language, and food are the three elements necessary for human beings if they are to continue living precisely as human beings. Jesus became present in a community (Church), language (Biblical Word), and food (Eucharist) because these elements are of central importance for human existence and continued human development. I suggest there was little choice in the matter because Jesus, in doing his Father's will, would have wanted to fulfill the archetypes of sacred presence.

No one will deny that food is necessary for life. We feed off the fruits, grains, vegetables, and animals we raise for meats. We slake our thirst with water, milk, wine, and a host of other liquids. Since human beings eat every day, if possible, it is not difficult to understand that food itself becomes a symbol of life that resonates with meaning structures or archetypes deep within the psyche.

We also feed off others. It has been shown repeatedly that a person is able to develop properly only within the environment of community, a nurturing environment wherein communication occurs on a regular basis. It is recounted that the Emperor Frederick II wanted to know what language is natural to human beings if they did not learn a language from others. He mused that perhaps children who were brought up never hearing a language would speak Hebrew, Greek, Latin, Arabic, or the language of their parents. He set up an experiment with several babies as subjects. "So he bade foster mothers and nurses to suckle the children, to bathe and wash them, but in no way to prattle with them or speak to them..." The outcome of the experiment foiled the emperor's will; all of the children died. In documented cases where children grew up in the care of animals, they were thoroughly feral and deranged. It has often been stated that human beings are inscribed within language, i.e., that they cannot be fully human without language. Language, of course, in learned within the context of family and community. The fundamental need for community and language also registers in psychic archetypes.

Sacred meals are celebrated in many cultures due to the influences of universal meaning structures or archetypes. These meals celebrate the solidarity of the community and are often used as occasions to reminisce about the reasons for the meal, the important events of the past upon which the sacred meal was established. "We reminisce," avers Edward Casey, "not only to savor but to understand, or re-understand, the past more adequately—where "understand" retains something of its root meaning of "standing under," gaining an intimate perspective not otherwise attainable. In reminiscing, we try to get back inside a given experience—to insinuate ourselves into it...—so as to come to know it better."[28]

The reasons for Jesus' presence in Church, Biblical Word, and Sacrament, upon reflection, are compelling. The risen Lord wished to get as close to us as possible so he elected modes of presence that are closest to us. Human nature itself institutes imperatives for community, language, and food. This is the same human nature, of course, that has been created by God. It is not at all surprising that Jesus would elect forms of presence congruent with the exigencies of the human nature that issued from divine creativity.

Real Presence. In order to develop an approach to explaining the presence of the risen Lord as *really* present in Church, Word, and Sacrament, it is also necessary to examine briefly the notion of presence. When someone sits across the table from me, that person is present to me face-to-face. In the narrow sense of the term, the person is really present to me. There are several kinds of face-to-face presences ranging from the kind of presence that obtains when someone speaks to me in anger to the kind of presence that occurs when someone embraces me and welcomes me home. The presence of husband and wife to one another in the act of intercourse certainly qualifies as a kind of real presence. But is face-to-face presence the only kind of real presence? I think not.

In a broader sense of the word presence, another person can be really present to me in a variety of ways. When someone speaks to me via a long distance telephone line, for example, that person is really present to me; the partner to the conversation is present to me in a very real way although he or she may be thousands of miles away. Vocal presence is surely a mode of real presence. Similarly, when I communicate with someone on the Internet, we are definitely present to one another in another mode of presence that must be classified as real. In some lesser sense of presence because it is not immediate in time, a friend is present to me in the exchange of letters with me. We may not be present to one another in the fullest meaning of "being present," i.e., face-to-face presence, but we are present voice-to-voice, mind-to-mind in the typescript of a personal computer or handwriting of a letter. I use these analogies to show that if we can be really present to other human beings in a variety of ways, so also can the risen Jesus be really present in the world in a variety of ways. If human beings can be really present to one another in various modes of presence—modes that constitute a hierarchy of presences—it is not at all unlikely that the risen and glorified Jesus controls modes of presence today in ways that are unfathomable to us.

One lexical meaning of presence relates to the space in the immediate vicinity of someone. To be present to another, in this sense of the word, one must be near the person physically. Another lexical meaning, however, is less rigid in its denotation. In this sense of the word, presence is simply the condition of being present to another. Nothing is stipulated as to the mode of presence by which the condition is fulfilled. Thus, it would seem, someone could be present to me when I remember the individual. In the wide sense of being present to someone, my memories of another person present the individual to me in the grammar of recollection. If my memories are especially vivid, might it not be considered that this is a form of real presence? When the broad use of the term *real* is used conjunctively with the general sense and less restrictive sense of the word *presence*, the notion of real presence becomes less obscure and, more to the point, more imaginable.

The image of the spiritual body of the resurrection is no more "strange" than the various depictions of body made by various theorists. The resurrection of Jesus, I think, cannot be proved as one would prove a theorem in geometry, but it can be shown to be compatible with human reason that is partnered with a paradigmatic religious imagination.

Affirming the Risen Jesus Today

Given all of the force of the modern secular imagination, an imagination that does not tolerate anything out of the commonplace much less anything supernatural, how do Christians today affirm the risen Jesus today? How are Christians able to "see through" the surface of reality to gain insight into the meaning of reality? How are Christians able to "see through" Church and Sacrament, and to "hear through" the Biblical Word to encounter the risen Jesus?

The ability to "see through" whatever veils the presence of the risen Jesus in the contemporary world is foremost a gift, a grace from God. Unless someone opens himself or herself to this gift, and unless the gift is bestowed, faith is impossible. While this mystery is utterly opaque, it is necessary nonetheless to state that the faith which allows anyone to interpret something imaginatively *as* something else or to see the risen Jesus in Church, Word, and Sacrament is bestowed on human beings gratuitously by God.

On the part of Christians, both love of the truth of divine revelation and trust in the God who reveals his truth in a million different ways is absolutely required. As is shown below in the consideration of Jesus' resurrection as an intellectual problem or a spiritual issue, the resurrection is fundamentally a spiritual issue. Belief in the resurrection must be exercised in the donation of self that occurs when someone loves and trusts another.

People are also enabled to believe in the resurrection of Jesus because of the natural dispositions to believe, dispositions that flow from the resurrection archetype. We expect and anticipate, quite naturally, to hail the Great Hero who has ventured forth in his suffering to combat the evil one and who will return from the place of the dead to the land of the living. The myth of the Great Hero is inscribed in our hearts. Those who are sensitive to what is true and good, all things being equal, are able to read the inscription.

The meaning structures in the collective unconscious of the race, generated over tens of thousands of years from the experience of being human in a world replete with symbols of death and resurrection, prompt us to believe in the Christian message. In final analysis, however, it is God who created the human psyche, the collective unconscious, and the world in which we dwell, a world rich in scenes and events that persuade us to think and imagine in resurrectional patterns. It seems that universal meaning structures or archetypes have forestructured human understanding in such a manner that not even the modern imagination, inhospitable as it is to Christianity, can shield itself against the power of the Christian imagination. *Anima naturaliter Christiana est.* The human psyche is naturally Christian. The subtlety of this truth, penned so long ago, can be appreciated even more today.

The Resurrection: An Intellectual or Spiritual Issue?

Is the resurrection of Jesus an issue that principally concerns the intellect, reason, and proof or is the matter referable more properly to spirituality. As an intellectual or apologetics problem, the issue of Jesus' resurrection may be held at arm's length. That is, anyone may speak of the resurrection intellectually without getting involved in a faith commitment to the truth of the resurrection. The issue becomes one of speculation, argumentation, and rational elaboration. As a purely apologetic problem, the resurrection of Jesus can also become a topic of debate.[29] As an intellectual/apologetic problem the issue raises this question: To what extent, if any, is Christian faith in the resurrection derived from human reason?

As noted in Chapter Three, Cardinal Newman, in one of his Oxford University sermons in 1839, commented that faith is often understood to be simply a moral act or act of will that depended beforehand on reason. Reason warrants, on the basis of ample evidence that the gospel comes from God; faith then embraces it. Newman presents what he calls a more scriptural account of the matter. "the act of faith is sole and elementary, and complete in itself, and depends on no process of mind previous to it..."[30] The person who accepts the Word of Life, according to Newman, does so on two grounds: 1)"the word of the human messenger and 2) the likelihood of the message."[31]

The human messenger who brings the Word of Life acts as God's instrument, an agent of divine revelation. The messengers are trustworthy and often bear within themselves the signs of holiness that identify them as God's instruments. Taken together as a body of baptized believers, it is possible to count the Church as an agent of divine revelation. The Church witnesses now, and has witnessed for centuries, that Jesus was raised bodily from the dead. This message challenges us. It is the message that elicits faith. The Christian message is deemed probable and worthy of belief, and the person who receives it "has a love for it, his love being strong though the testimony is weak. He has a keen sense of the intrinsic excellence of the message, of its desirableness, of its likeness to what it seems to him Divine Goodness would vouchsafe, did he vouchsafe any, of the need of a revelation, and its probability. Thus faith is the reasoning of a religious mind or of what scripture calls a right or renewed heart..."[32]

However, faith in the resurrection of Jesus, a mature faith, is not the outcome of speculative reasoning or philosophical disputes. The resurrection of Jesus was not posed by the apostles as a proposition that could be discovered by reason. The resurrection was not preached as an academic conundrum. On the contrary, the resurrection of Jesus was heralded as a divine saving deed, as God's definitive Word in human history. It was to be affirmed or denied as such and not as a philosopical puzzle. Those who were of a right heart would hear the inner testimony of the divine origin of the resurrection; those who were not of a right heart would not be swayed by such a testimony. The only time that Paul's announcement of the resurrection was construed as a speculative philosophical doctrine by the Stoics and Epicureans of Athens, the good news received an uneven reception. Some Athenians scoffed at the message, others wanted to discuss the matter further, and a few became believers (Acts 17: 16-34).

This does not imply that discussions of the significance and meaning of the resurrection are improper. While faith is not the offspring of reason, what is accepted in faith must at least not be unreasonable. God expects us to use the reason he gave us in its proper turn. God wants us to be faithful but not credulous. Faith needs reason, in fact, to save it from being superstitious. Faith seeks understanding and reasoning is employed in this search. "Faith seeking understanding," is the traditional definition of theology. "Faith seeking understanding," of course, is essentially different from "reason seeking faith" although human reasoning, in recognizing its own limitations, can turn the soil for the seed of faith.

Perhaps there is a stage in the faith development of nearly everyone when the resurrection is foremost, *de facto*, an intellectual problem. For this reason, debates and speculations about the resurrection of Jesus should not be ruled out absolutely, although there is a danger that some who accept Jesus's resurrection may think this affirmation is the end result of their own reasoning and not God's gift. A mature faith always understands that its provenance, inevitably and ultimately, is traceable to the loving kindness of an all-gracious God.

Concluding Remarks

The resurrection of Jesus is primarily a matter for religious faith. It is doubtful at this point in the present course of events that any kind of exact history which ignores the Christ of faith can result in a credible account of the Jesus of history. For the apostles, the resurrection of Jesus was something that occurred in the objective order of history. It is a big stretch to claim on the basis of Biblical evidence and evidence of Christian tradition that Jesus was experienced subjectively by the apostles although he was not actually risen and did not actually manifest himself to those elected to hear the good news. A recent book that makes the resurrection a mere psychological experience on the part of the apostles is Gerd Luedemann's interpretive effort.[33] More important, however, than the book itself is Carl Braaten's estimable comments about the author's underlying frame of reference. "Luedemann's reduction of the resurrection narratives to pscyhological experiences is one of many current examples of theologians conforming to a thoroughgoing secular view of history and reality. In our secular modern worldview there is no God to act in history, and faith has no objective basis in historical events by which God brings life out of death. Since belief in the resurrection of the dead does not fit with our secularized mindset, Jesus' resurrection must be explained away as a product of purely human activity."[34]

To believe that Jesus actually rose from the dead and manifested himself to the apostles and others is also to believe that the course of human events we call history belongs to a God who acts in history, a God whose Word was definitively uttered in the event of the risen Jesus. Belief in the resurrection is possible only within the faith perspective that views history as a dialogue between human beings and the God for whom all things are possible.

To believe that Jesus actually rose from the dead is not far from the belief that he is really present today in the Church, Biblical Word, and Eucharist. This is to say that Jesus, the Word of God, is present today within the events of human history, communicating with his people and with the world at large.

Notes to Chapter 5

1. Mary Warnock, "Religious Imagination," *Religious Imagination,* ed. James Mackey (Edinburgh: Edinburgh University Press, 1986), 147.

2. E.P. Sanders, *The Historical Figure of Jesus* (New York: Penguin Books USA, 1993), 280.

3. John P. Meier, *A Marginal Jew: Rethinking the Historical Jesus* (New York: Doubleday, vol. 1, 1991), 13.

4. Raymond E. Brown, *The Death of the Messiah: From Gethsemane to Grave* (New York: Doubleday, vol. 1, 1994), xii.

5. Juan Luis Segundo, *The Historical Jesus of the Synoptics,* trans. John Drury (Maryknoll, NY: Orbis Books, 1985), 166.

6. Marinus de Jonge, *Christology in Context: The Earliest Christian Response to Jesus* (Philadelphia: The Westminster Press, 1988), 186–187.

7. Pheme Perkins, *Resurrection: New Testament Witness and Contemporary Reflection* (Garden City, NY: Doubleday, 1984), 255.

8. Marcus Borg, *Jesus: A New Vision* (San Francisco: Harper and Row. 1987), 185.

9. William F. Ong and James A. Walther, "Introduction," *I Corinthians: A New Translation,* The Anchor Bible (New York: Doubleday, 1986), 120–121.

10. See Bruce Winter, "I Corinthians," eds. G. Wenham G., J. Motyer, J., D. Carson, and France, R., *New Bible Commentary* (Downers Grove, IL : InterVarsity, 1994), 1161–1163.

11. Ong and Walther, 273.

12. Earl Mac Cormac, *A Cognitive Theory of Metaphor* (Cambridge, MA: The MIT Press, 1985), 207.

13. Ibid., 208. It is very much beyond the purposes of this chapter to provide even an introductory treating of metaphor as truth. Readers interested in learning more about this topic would do well to read Mac Cormac's interesting book.

14. Janet Martin Soskice, *Metaphor and Religious Language* (New York: Oxford University Press, Clarendon Paperback, 1988), 149.

15. Richard Kugelman, "The First Letter to the Corinthians," eds. Raymond E. Brown, Joseph A. Fitzmyer, and Roland E. Murphy, *The Jerome Biblical Commentary* (Englewood Cliffs, NJ: Prentice Hall, 1968), 271.

16. Daniel Taylor, *The Myth of Certainty* (Waco, TX: Word Books, 1986), 111.

17. Malcolm Muggeridge, *Jesus Rediscovered* (Garden City: Doubleday and Co., 1969), ix.

18. Ibid., 271.

19. Raymond E. Brown , *The Death of the Messiah: From Gethsemane to the Grave* (New York : Doubleday Publishing Co., 1994), 9.

20. Walter J. Ong,. *The Presence of the Word: Some Prologomena for Cultural and Religious History* (Minneapolis: University of Minnesota Press, 1991), 179–185.

21. Ibid., 188–189.

22. Ibid., 271.

23. Augustine of Hippo, *St. Augustine: Confessions,* trans. R. Pine-Coffin, (New

York: Penguin Books, 1984), 177–178.

24. Jerome Murphy-O'Connor, "I Corinthians," in *The New Jerome Biblical Commentary,* Raymond E. Brown, Joseph A. Fitzmeyer, and Roland E.Murphy, (Englewood Cliffs, NJ: Prentice Hall Publishing Co., 1990). 809.

25. William Barclay, *The Letters to the Corinthians* (Philadelphia: Westminster Press, 1956), 103.

26. Ibid., 103–104.

27. Salimbene, "The Emperor Frederick II," eds. James Ross and Mary McLaughlin, *The Portable Medieval Reader* (New York: Viking Press, 1955), 366.

28. Edward S. Casey, *Remembering: A Phenomenological Study* (Bloomington & Indianapolis: Indiana University Press, Midland Book, 1987), 117.

29. See Gary Habermas and Anthony Flew, ed. Terry L. Miethe, *Did Jesus Rise from the Dead: The Resurrection Debate* (San Francisco: Harper and Row, 1987).

30. John Henry Newman, "The Nature of Faith in Relation to Reason," in *Sermons and Discourses* (New York: Longmans, Green and Company, 1949), 326.

31. Ibid., 326.

32. Ibid., 327. In another sermon in the book entitled "Secret Faults" in the same volume Newman writes: "The inward witness to the truth lodged in our hearts is a match for the most learned infidel or sceptic that ever lived..." p. 22. I view this inward witness as the prompting of the Holy Spirit resonating in the deep meaning structure known as the resurrection archetype.

33. Gerd Luedemann, *The Resurrection of Jesus: History, Experience, Theology* (Philadelphia: Fortress Press, 1994).

34. Carl E. Braaten, "Can We Still be Christians?" in *Pro Ecclesia, 4, 4, 1995, 397.*

Appendix A
THE ORIGIN OF PAGAN RESURRECTION MYTHS

Myths that feature the resurrection of dead gods or goddesses were produced in prehistoric times. Only a very foolish person would attempt to explain the provenance of these myths with certitude and precision. Prehistoric times, by definition, are beyond the ken of contemporary men and women. The most anyone can do to make the issue intelligible is provide a plausible explanation or interpretation of the creation and development of these stories. My purposes in this appendix, then, are quite modest.

I proposed earlier that those who first heard the Good News of Jesus' resurrection were prepared to receive this announcement favorably for two reasons. First, because of their conscious familiarity with pagan resurrection myths, the proclamation of Jesus' resurrection was not discerned as something entirely incredible. In their own way, pagan resurrection myths conveyed a pivotal sense of the appropriateness of the general notion of resurrection. This sense of the relevance of the concept of resurrection for human life probably derived from the aesthetic judgment of individuals and not so much from highly logical speculative arguments. Aesthetic judgment, I suggest, is based on an intuitive sense of what is right, seemly, harmonious, and fitting. People operate out of their aesthetic judgment and the feelings derived from their life experiences (as contrasted to judgment based on second-hand fact, so to speak, and logic) far more often than most of us wish to admit. Aesthetic judgment also emphasizes the place of affect and emotion in the act of judgment much more than the speculative judgment that is based mainly on facts we secure from books and logic.

Second, those individuals in the beginnings of Christianity who were inclined to accept of the Good News were of such a tendency because of their experiences of resurrection motifs in the world of nature. The character of this experience, I believe, was largely subliminal, that is, the experience of resurrection motifs in the world that was the object of human experience was more intuitively insightful than intellectually abstract. Most individuals did not experience discursively the abstract ideas of death and resurrection from their falling asleep each night and arising the next morning. What they experienced was an image that lurked beneath the level of conscious advertence. They experienced a sense of sleeping and rising as thematic for a human existence that was confronted by death frequently and dramatically. In any event, out of these experiences over thousands of years of human experience the resurrection archetype took form in the human psyche. The proclamation of Jesus' resurrection resonated in the profound reaches of the unconscious of those who listened to the promptings of the resurrection archetype.

It must be noted further that Jesus was also proclaimed, early on, as the Word of God through whom all things came into being. "In the beginning was the Word, and the Word was with God, and the Word was God. All things came into being through him, and without him not one thing came into being." (John 1:1-3). "And the Word became flesh and lived among us, and we have seen his glory, the glory as of a father's only son, full of grace and truth." (John 1: 14). Now the very notion of the world's creation conveys the image of coming into being from non-being, a sort of coming-into-life from the void of chaos that resembles death. It was this same Jesus, the Word made flesh, who was present at, and involved in, the world's coming into being. *All of the resurrection motifs in the world bespeak the world's original awakening from chaos to cosmos.* It would not at all have been difficult to accept Jesus, the Word of God, as risen Lord as long as a believer associated Jesus' resurrection with the power that raised the entire universe from the chaos that approximated nothingness and placed resurrection motifs everywhere in the created world.

In sum, early Christians affirmed the resurrection of Jesus as the beginning of a new creation because they were familiar with the idea of resurrection as found in pagan myths, because they associated Jesus with the divine creative Word uttered in the first creation, and because they experienced thousands of times the resurrection motifs that abounded in the created world.

Appendix Outline

What I wish to address in this appendix, in more detail that I did in Chapter Three, are the dynamics underlying the construction of pagan resurrection myths. I hypothesize that there are four elements that came together in the creative process:

1. An intuitive understanding of the resurrectional structure of the created world. This understanding constituted the very foundation of the process by which resurrection myths were created.
2. An experience of the heroic as exemplified in a local hero and the development of a local saga based on the hero's exploits.
3. Development of the great monomyth of the hero who goes out, meets a challenge, and returns triumphant to bestow favors on those who awaited his return.
4. The redaction of multiple local sagas into regional or territorial resurrection myths

The Resurrectional Structure of the Created World

Mythmakers did not create the stories out of nothing. The basis for myths, the character that gave myths their verisimilitude, was the resurrectional structure of the created world. The intuition of the resurrectional structure of the natural world arose spontaneously in the psyches of the artists who created myths that featured a resurrectional, revival, or renewal theme. I remember once asking an artist who lectured on the creative impulses associated with artistic production to describe how he determined what to sculpt. Allow me to paraphrase his answer. "I don't know," he responded, "what I am almost compelled to sculpt is what bubbles up from within my soul. The model is simply *there* in my heart and minds-eye." I learned from his response that the essence of art is not the ability to draw, paint, sculpt, play a musical instrument, and so forth, but instead the capacity for artistic intuition, the readiness to grasp completely (intellectually and affectively) what presents itself to consciousness after its voyage from the unconscious.

The artists who fashioned resurrection myths no doubt had experienced what was available for all humankind to experience, but perhaps they were closer to the rhythms of the created world. Because they were artists, perhaps, they were more sensitive to the themes that were enacted in nature. They perceived the cycles of vegetation. Seeds were placed into the ground. They appeared to die but unaccountably produced new life in the Spring. Such phenomena were remarkable because they overwhelmed the human imagination with wonder. It seemed as if the processes of the world were structured in such a manner as to restore—on a consistent basis—what was dead and decaying into something vital and flourishing.

The mythmakers also experienced climatic and solar cycles. They knew that each year the earth itself, in the temperate regions, must grow cold and die. The sun itself would withdraw gradually during the year until it too seemed to die. But then there was always a glorious rebirth of the sun and that brought warmer weather, weather that appeared to work hand in glove with cycles of vegetation. The sun was, what everyone in the Roman world would later hail as *Sol Invictus*, the Unconquerable Sun. For those who worshiped the sun, their friendly god who graciously brought light and warmth to his people, was indeed worthy of praise and veneration. This god displayed his might each year. He grew old and seemed to draw away from his people in something resembling death, but he arose again to new life.

Each daily cycle of sunrise and sunset offered the mythmakers a closer lesson of what occurred in large scale each year. Each day the sun arose from either sleep or death in the wondrous east, marched through the skies at midday, and settled back into the gloom of night. How frightening it must have been very early in human experience when the sun descended into the place of the dead! Would this resplendent god return bringing light and warmth? Humankind soon learned to trust this unconquerable deity. And mythmakers found that something bubbled up in their souls as a precipitate of their experiences: the outlines of a story of death and resurrection.

Mythmakers also watched by night with tens of thousands of others. They witnessed the march of the constellations across the night sky. Some constellations that seemed to outline figures of living beings were born in one area of the starry vault and exited or died in another area. The moral of the story told by the night skies was the lesson that the hope which welled up in the human breast was not in vain. Veritable promises are given in the signs presented by this vast cosmos wherever we look! The universe itself bespeaks the message that death shall have no final victory over us.

Mythmakers also experienced resurrection in the fortunes of their tribal families. How many uncounted fashioners of resurrection myths knew what it was like to experience the seeming downfall of the tribal community from famine, beasts, or other humans who set themselves against the tribe as enemies? Yet somehow these artists lived to tell a story of resurrection and revival. The end seemed near enough, but the rains came just in time, the beasts were slain by brave men of the tribe who would be forever celebrated, enemies were unexpectedly overturned by the village warriors, or they were decimated by a fever, or they found, at the last moment, more profitable concerns than warfare.

Finally, mythmakers must have experienced a sense of psychological death and resurrection. They must have experienced the mood of being thrust toward death and nothingness and, subsequently, a resurrectional reversal of this mood. Their moods of depression and despondency were overturned by modes of elation and delight. The mood that all was dust and ashes was itself a kind of anticipation of death. The mood of being fully alive and full of exhilaration, on the other hand, was an anticipation of rebirth into a new life.

The structure of the created world discloses motifs of death and resurrection to such a degree that the discernment of these motifs constitutes a universal human experience. From the vast expanses of the starry skies to the equally great expanses of the human soul, reality fairly shouts a message that encourages hope. Years ago I pondered a text from a now-forgotten volume on Eastern religion: "The fragrance of promise is in the air." For those who know how to discern, promises of a transformed life after a seeming irrevocable demise are everywhere we look. Promises abound. These promises, I would argue, served as a basis for the creation of resurrection myths.

(I have offered in these pages examples of death-resurrection motifs that occur in seven different aspects of the world. There are many more examples that range from the dramatic to the commonplace. Death-resurrection motifs abound almost everywhere. For example, the first-born son of a family runs away from home and begins to live a life of dissolution. He becomes a drug addict. Just when it seems the son will be forever lost, he experiences a change of heart that leads to a new life. He is raised from the death of addiction and dissolution, and is restored to the life of his family. Another example, harsh words are exchanged between a married couple. Feelings are hurt. A shadow is cast in the home that hovers over both husband and wife. Life seems to have drained out of their union. Words of apology are spoken. The pall is lifted. Their common life is raised from the depths to a new joy. Can a resurrection motif actually be found within the context of something as ordinary as a marital tift? For the couple who argued and made up, their shared experience speaks of death and resurrection, perhaps, in the language they best understand. It does not take much imagination, I suggest, to draw up a lengthy list of the motifs that point to the resurrectional structure that dominates the world of human experience).

An Experience of the Heroic

A new kind of experience by mythmakers comprised another ingredient that went into resurrection myths. Mythmakers no doubt encountered heroes in their lives or, at the very least, stories of local heroes. They knew a fearless member of the tribe, perhaps, who went out alone to combat an insatiable beast that was decimating the tribal community. The hero went out of the village precincts armed with a knife and spear, and a plentiful store of courage. The hero trusted the gods of his tribe to deliver the trembling members of the tribe from evil and to grant him victory over the beast. A few days after the hero's departure from the village, a terrible commotion was heard on the outskirts of the settlement. Finally, the roaring of the beast subsided. Shortly thereafter the bedraggled hero returned to his community covered in blood and carrying the head of a lion. The conqueror was celebrated as hero of the tribe.

This experience of the heroic combined with the image of death and resurrection in the imaginations of the mythmakers. A hero goes out to certain death to deliver his people from danger. Remarkably, he returns from his voyage toward death covered in blood but nonetheless fully alive. His life, in fact, has been transformed by his victory over a seemingly unconquerable adversary. The story of the hero is sung over the tribe's campfires. After several generations, the story changes somewhat. As the time of his death approached, according to the song, the gods of the tribe proclaimed the hero to be immortal. The hero was taken into the divine realm as a co-equal of the gods.

The above scenario, of course, is a story of what might have happened in a particular village and within the sacred traditions of the people who lived in that village. A local hero saves his people at the risk of his own life. There are many variations on the theme, however. The hero goes out to hunt in a time of famine and trespasses the lair of a wild animal in search of food. As he leaves the village it is widely accepted that he faces certain death. He returns victorious, however, and laden with fresh meat from the kill to grant the boon of life to the members of the tribe. In the sacred sagas and traditions of the tribe, in later accounts of the hero's exploits, he is apotheosized and taken to live with the gods. The element of the heroic is interweaved with the motif of death and resurrection.

This linkage of the motifs of death and resurrection with the theme of heroism at the local level, at the plane of the tribal community, could have been accomplished even when the hero was not victorious. Suppose the brave hero ventured forth from the village into the precincts of a wild animal that was threatening the villagers. He engaged the beast in a life and death struggle but lost this struggle after a intrepid fight witnessed from afar by other warriors who accompanied the hero. The wild beast may have eventually died of its wounds, but the hero was killed outright.

No doubt celebratory songs would be sung over many campfires in honor of the hero who lost his life in the service of his fellows. There is equally little doubt that such a narrative would be continued over many generations due to the spectacular character the encounter between the hero (whose memory was ritualized in the repetition of the campfire narrative) and the animal (who came to stand for all that was malevolent). Indeed, as time went on, the saga would develop a new ending. After the hero had been slain, the gods took him into the midst because of his action on behalf of the tribe. The hero, as the sun who dies in the west but is born again each morning in the east, was reborn into a divine realm. Given the resurrection archetype in the unconscious reaches of the psyches of tribal members, an archetype that was precisely there due to the universal experiences by the tribe of the death/resurrection motifs in the created world, there could be no other conclusion about a hero who was so brave and so beloved of his people.

Development of the Great Monomyth

Joseph Campbell summed up the elements of the Great Monomyth in these words: "A hero ventures forth from the world of common day into a region of supernatural wonder: fabulous forces are there encountered and a decisive victory is won: the hero comes back from this mysterious adventure with the power to bestow boons on his fellow man."[1] The Great Monomyth is so-called because it is found, in one variation or another, in most cultures. The word "monomyth" was itself taken by Campbell from James Joyce's *Finnegan's Wake* and suggests an archetypal myth that serves as pattern for all myths.

It probably did not take long for most people to realize, after they met individuals from other tribal communities, that they shared the elements of the same myth of the hero. The experience of resurrection motifs in the natural world, combined with the memory of some actual tribal hero, led ineluctably to the development of the Great Monomyth. Notice, I locate the origins of this common-shared myth not in any arcane innate knowledge but instead in the essentially similar life experiences of various peoples. The myth originated out of experiences of resurrection motifs in nature combined with experiences of the heroic. It was this myth of the hero that served as paradigm for the development of regional or territorial resurrection myths. And since myths of the hero, all containing essentially similar features, were universally present in ancient cultures, my inference is not that human beings were born with the myth in their unconscious but that the meaning structures of the unconscious were formed out of universally shared experiences of the heroic.

Redaction of Local Sagas into Territorial Myths

As people gradually understood that they shared resurrection myths involving various local heroes, it would not have been long before some mythmakers and singers of songs redacted the resurrection myths of individual tribes into a larger myth that could be celebrated over a relatively wide territory. Territorial myths, for example, would be the resurrection myth of Tammuz who dominated the religious practices of Babylonians and other Semites outside of Judaism. Adonis, of course, was for the Greeks what Tammuz was for the Semitic peoples. Each of these territorial myths contained common elements and each, in turn, featured elements that were specific to Semites and Greeks respectively. Regional or territorial resurrection myths, it seems, developed in respect to language groups. Language is at the center of any culture. Thus, the figure of Tammuz played a central role in the mythology of many who spoke Semitic dialects; Adonis was a major figure in the mythology of many Greek-speaking peoples. Each principal language group in the Mediterranean basin had its own resurrection myth; the details of the mythic narrative varied according to local custom.

The Natural Origin of Resurrection Myths

What I mean by the natural origin of pagan resurrection myths is this: The world was created by God in such a manner that resurrection motifs abound. The human psyche was created by God in such a manner that natural experiences of these motifs effected a resurrection meaning structure in the deep reaches of the pscyhe. Human beings were created by God in such a manner that heroes would arise at various times to face death for the deliverance of their tribal communities. The "fit" or correspondence of the resurrection meaning structure with the ideal of the hero gave rise to pagan resurrection myths. The world was created in such a way by God that resurrection myths occurred naturally. In some way, I suggest, the Creator of the world is responsible for so-called pagan resurrection myths since the Creator is responsible for the resurrection motifs in nature and for the psychic mechanisms that processed the human experiences of these motifs and experiences of the heroic.

Pagan resurrection myths, for those who are able to discern, foreshadow the central event of God's dialogue with his creatures, the resurrection of Jesus. *This is to say that pagan resurrection myths, in their own limited way, were vehicles of God's revelation.* What is pagan, then, is not to be disparaged as if there was nothing worthy in paganism. There is in paganism and in pagan resurrection myths a bestowal of insight by the God who created pagans as well as Christians.

The insight granted to the pagans by God prepared the way for the resurrection of Jesus, the actual resurrection that validated mythic resurrections as somehow meaningful. In the resurrection of Jesus, all of the abounding death-resurrection motifs in the created world are shown as somehow revelatory of divine purpose. In God's decisive Word-Event spoken in human history—in the raising of Jesus from the dead—all of the obscure whispered promises of a life beyond with God that were heard in the depths of unnumbered human psyches are authenticated somehow as the veritable whispers of God himself. All human experiences of death-resurrection somehow begin to make sense when these experiences are viewed through the lens of Jesus' resurrection.

Note to Appendix A

1. Joseph Campbell, *The Hero with a Thousand Faces* (Princeton University Press: Princeton, N.J.) 1968, 30.

Appendix B
THE BODILY RESURRECTION
OF JESUS

Someone once told me that it would be far easier for him to believe in the survival of Jesus' soul than his bodily resurrection from the dead. The notion of a bodily resurrection seems to bespeak a primitive mentality. The ancient Egyptians, after all, placed food and furniture in the tombs of the Pharaohs for their use in the afterlife. They preserved the bodies of the dead Pharaohs as if expecting their physical survival in the realm of the dead. Nothing suggests the finality and irrevocability of death, my friend continued, than a corpse and its eventual disintegration under the leveling destruction brought by the passage of time.

It is no doubt true that there is something final about a dead body. And it is true that most ancient peoples, from what we can deduce from funeral rituals, believed in some kind of bodily persistence after death in the afterlife. And, we must admit it, there seems to be (at first glance) something archaic about the Christian belief in the bodily resurrection of Jesus and the Christian hope in the final resurrection of all who died. Of course, what is archaic sometimes speaks to us out of deep human meaning structures that have been constituted on the basis of universal human experience. Without exploring these archetypes again, it is sufficient to say that most people apprise the post-death survival of a soul or shade as a kind of wispy and insubstantial form of existence. The only existence we know as real is a bodily existence. Anything less than a bodily existence seems less than a real existence.

Various notions of body are explored in this appendix. While it may seem, again at first glance, that everyone knows with ample clarity what a body is, the truth is that the meaning of the human body is obscure and mysterious when we begin to define it. To assume that the meaning of the body is a simple matter is to have given the issue little thought. And if understandings of the physical body are not totally clear, attempts to penetrate the meaning of a "risen body" seem destined for failure. A "risen body" is not simply naturally mysterious; it is religiously or supernaturally mysterious. That there have been many different understandings of what constitutes a body, and a "risen body," can be documented well enough by reference to Caroline Walker Bynum's monumental and important work on notions of the resurrection of the body in Western Christianity between 200 and 1336 A.D. The one theme that emerges from a reading of her book, despite different notions of bodily resurrection, is that to be human is to be an embodied person.[1] Nor should one neglect to read Benedict Ashley's classic work on humanist and Christian theologies of the body. The book not only discusses different notions of "body" but also the phenomenal body, the mystical body, the resurrected body, the spiritual body, and the glorified body.[2]

The present consideration of various interpretive understandings of the body is modest given the space limitations of an appendix. The following discussion of the bodily resurrection of Jesus, however, may emphasize the fact that those who believe in the bodily resurrection believe in an event that is mysterious and not easily defined. This is as it should be since a divine mystery, even when it occurs within the framework of human history, is likely to require—to understate the matter greatly—more than an easy explanation. Those who reject the bodily resurrection of Jesus, on the other hand, may find the following paragraphs helpful in that they will be enabled to articulate precisely what kind of bodily resurrection they decline to accept.

Given the obscurity that surrounds the notion of "body," it seems just as difficult at times to reject the bodily resurrection of Jesus as to accept the Good News first announced by the apostles.

Meanings of Body

A brief but helpful review of the changing meanings of the body during human history is provided by Antoine Vergote.[3] Vergote's elaboration is sometimes difficult to follow; his brief journey through history does suggest, however, that the meanings attached to the concept of body are complex and varied.

Vergote mentions the study of the meaning of the human body is important for Christians because it is particularly for them that the religious destiny of the body is central. He goes on to state that the concept of body is "foremost an historical idea which has been formed over centuries of observation and thought."[4] It is crucial, I believe, to come to terms with the historicity of the concept of the body, that is, it is crucial to be aware that our contemporary popular notion of the body has been shaped by centuries of reflection and that there may be multiple legitimate descriptive definitions of the body, none of them completely exhaustive of the richness of the term. As with the notion of "historical event," there may be more involved linguistically than theologically when we speak of the bodily resurrection of Jesus. In addition to the problematics stemming from the use of language, there may also be several levels of interpretation of the meaning of body. To speak of the body from the standpoint of weight, for example, is not the same as speaking of the body from the perspective of height, aesthetics, medical status, or state of development. In other words, there are many difficulties associated with any explanation of the human body.

Plato, according to Vergote, elaborated the first systematic formulation of the body. He understood the person to be a composite of body and soul. The soul is the animating principle of the body. There was no doubt which of the two elements was the most important. The body was the prison of the soul. The body was mortal and the soul immortal. The body was as changeable as the material from which it was made; the soul was as spiritual as the ideas it contemplated. For Plato the body (*soma*) is a kind of tomb (*sema*) for the soul. Many religious thinkers for hundreds of years followed Platonic thought on the body and associated the soul with that aspect of the person that was immortal and redeemable. Many Christians think of the immortal human soul, despite the fact that inevitably they must admit (if they are true to the Christian tradition} that on the day the Lord returns, the body will rise again in the imitation of the risen Christ.

Aristotle, the most notable student of Plato, rejected his teacher's view of the body. Aristotle taught there was a unity between body and soul. The soul, in fact, was the internal form of the body, a form that organized the matter of the body. In this perspective, the body has a positive role to play in its union with the soul. It is only through the instrumentality of the body that a person experiences material reality and learns. Still, Aristotle maintained that only the soul survives after death. The body, far from being a tomb of the soul, is valuable because all knowledge comes through the senses; the body serves the soul well and deserves respect.

At this point in the article, Vergote observes that the Biblical and Christian notion of the body was quite different from Platonic or Aristotelian ideas. He points out that there is no semantic equivalent in Hebrew for the Greek term for body, *soma*. "In a Semitic context one cannot conceive of the body as a circumscribed totality because the bodily organs—heart, kidneys, lungs—metaphorically represent, under a relational aspect, the ensemble of rapports that man maintains with others, with the world, and with God. In this sense, man is not an individualized entity but an ensemble of diversely qualified relations. He is not someone who has a body but (someone) whose existence is corporal."[5] It was possible, according to F. J. Taylor "to use the word body with the meaning of self, person, personality, or whole man, and indeed neither Hebrew nor Greek had words to express these concepts."[6]

Human beings enjoy corporal existence and all of their relationships are referable to this bodily existence. Anyone's final release from life at the hand of God must entail not simply the deliverance of a soul, but also the rescue of the body which mediated all of the individual's relationships forged during the person's life, relationships that taken together accounted for the individual's integral identity. While a photo on a driver's licence can be said to *identify* someone in respect to outward appearance, each person's *fundamental identity* can be found only in the ensemble of relationships experienced by that individual during his or her lifetime. The body is, at least, the instrumental means of forging these relationships.

The soul in the Hebrew Bible (*nephesh*) at death leaves the mortal flesh (*sarx*) and does not survive. The notion of *sarx* bears multiple connotations including the unregenerate state of fallen humanity (e.g., Romans 7:5), the observable external dimensions of things (Colossians 2:1), and other meanings. *Soma, nephesh,* and *sarx* are the essential constitutive elements of present human life. As can be easily grasped, there is a profound difference between the Greek and Biblical ideas of body and soul.

Descartes and the Body

The next development or change in the concept of body took place in the 17th century. Rene Descartes wished to establish a philosophy that provided conclusions as certain as geometrical inferences. He based his philosophy entirely on the proposition *Cogito, ergo sum.* "I think, therefore I am." This "I" of which Descartes wrote—and this is crucial to understanding him—is immediate to its own self without the mediation of the body. This fateful belief served as the basis for many different strands of modern philosophy. What is implied about the body in this understanding of "I" was also portentous. The body was objectified completely; it became a machine in the minds of those who accepted the basic premise of Cartesian philosophy. The body of a living man differed from that of a dead man in the same way a wound-up watch differed from a watch when the principle of its movement is absent.

These results occurred as a result of Descartes' thinking. First, biology and medicine began looking at the body in terms of bio-machinery, that is biology and medicine began viewing the body in really more productive ways. Second, the ancient distinction between body and soul "hardened," according to Vergote. And finally, "discoveries about the physical regulation of the body eventually eliminated any interest in the soul as a principle of intellection in the body."[7] The human being became viewed increasingly and principally as an animated body.

From the standpoint of phenomenology, the author quotes Gabriel Marcel. Marcel noted that from one perspective someone can say " I *am* a body" yet from another vantage point that person can also say, " I *have* a body." The body, then, is the frontier between being and having. My existence, in other words, means *being* a body in a world containing other bodies and, simultaneously, *having* a body. We can view our bodies as the locus of our subjectivity on the one hand, and the locus of our objectivity on the other. We are subjects/objects in the world due to our bodies. How this is so is a great mystery.

Vergote next takes up considerations of the body from the standpoint of anthropology and psychology. What sets human beings apart from other animals is the lack of instinctual responses characteristic of other animals and a kind of plasticity that allows human beings to transcend their environment. What is more, this remarkable plasticity always seems to be associated with language. Quoting Arnold Gehlen, the author observes that at a particular time in the history of the world words and ideas must have fairly exuded from the brain and body. Equipped with words human beings were able to take charge of their own lives.[8]

Vergote suggests the body must be studied in terms of "three language chains." There is the language of objective body (the corporal machine), psychological language (the lived body), and ontological language (the body of the "flesh" in the sense used by the philosopher Merleau-Ponty). "The body, both interiorly and relationally affective, is well expressed by another Hebraic term for flesh (*basar*)."[9] *Basar* can mean a manifestation of a soul (Genesis 2:7) or the entire human being (Psalm 16:

9-10).[10] This suggests that the body is a center of action for the corporal and physical side of being human, a center of action for the psyche, and a center of action, as flesh, for the development of affective relationships.

The psychic body is discussed further by the author. Vergote cites a case study offered by the philosopher-therapist Jacques Lacan. It seems a man suffered from writer's cramp. The man was a Moslem. Under analysis the individual admitted that his father had once been accused of being a thief. This was particularly distressing for the man with the cramp because he was reared according to Islamic law which required the amputation of the hand of a convicted thief. The interpretation of this situation was fairly easy. The body "spoke" in the writer's cramp and "said" it would accept—in substitution for the father—the sanction of the law. Somehow the psychic body was able to express thoughts symbolically about which the man was not conscious. Vergote states "At the very least these observations indicate that the body is not uniquely regulated by biological structures alone but that it is susceptible to incarnating, in the strong sense of the world, the order of language."[11]

The complexity of what Vergote calls the psychic body is the result of the imbrication between the order of life and the order of language. What the author means is that what occurs in the psychic body is a consequence of the overlap between the experiences of the animated body and the active capacity for language and thought.

The Body According to Henri Bergson

In the same journal in which was published Vergote's article there appeared, over three years later, an article by John Mullarkey on contemporary philosophies of the body and the idea of the body in the philosophy of Henri Bergson. Bergson's concept of the body is the sole theme of the article relevant to present purposes.

Bergson observed that the body may be considered in two ways. First, from the standpoint of quantitative science it is something that can be touched; the body has a definite form and dimension largely independent of our choosing. The visual image of the body would indicate its presence. If we truly wished to ascertain its reality, however, we would also test its presence by means of touch. Second, if we think of the body as that "to which consciousness applies itself, it is coextensive with our consciousness, it comprises all we perceive, it reaches to the stars."[12] Consciousness as it applies itself, is no less real than quantitative extension in space.

The body that can be ascertained confidently by means of the visual and tactile senses is the "body for the world." That is, its definite form and dimension is available to the senses of others. The body which is the instrument of consciousness, on the other hand, is available only to ourselves. This is the "body for itself." This "body for itself" is a center of action in that its perceptions of the world around it pay heed to the possible actions of the world upon it and, likewise, actions that are taken in response to the events that occur in the world. These perceptions also create a world for the perceiver that is constituted of other "bodies for the world," bodies that offer images of opportunity and danger for the perceiver. The author concludes the article with the idea that the body has incompatible properties; it is duplicitous. The body, according to Bergson, has two manifestations. The "body for others" is a body among other bodies with definite form and dimension; it is also a "body for itself" that is coextensive with consciousness. In the former instance, the body is connected to the earth; in the latter instance, the body is isolated from the earth because, in the words of Bergson, "it reaches to the stars."

Bergson's distinction between a person's "body for itself" and "body for others" is difficult to understand because we are accustomed to think in terms of body and soul, and not in terms of Aristotle's entelechy (the principle of a living body that is much less spiritual than our notion of soul) and his idea of body (which is considerably less corporeal than our modern notion of body. Quantity and quality were distinct, but not separate realities in Aristotelian thought. Perhaps Bergson's notions of "body for itself" and "body for others" can be understood only by those who make an effort to conceptualize the human person as a unitary being composed of distinct "principles" of existence that are inseparable as long as we live.[13]

Some Inferences

As a result of the foregoing reflections, I suggest that three inferences can be legitimately made. First, denials of the possibility of Jesus's resurrection on the basis of crudely conceived ideas about the body must be denied. The notion of body is far too complex to allow the thesis that the resurrection of Jesus is impossible because bodies simply cannot be raised from the dead according to contemporary scientific understanding. The truth is that many respected thinkers in the course of history have described the body in different ways, many of which were not compatible with the reigning paradigm that governed empirical science. Indeed, given some contemporary understandings of matter itself, the notion of bodily resurrection is not at all unthinkable.

The celebrated theoretical physicist Freeman Dyson, in his Gifford Lectures, described matter as "the way particles behave when a large number of them are lumped together." He went on to say that theoretical physicists "have learned that matter is weird stuff. It is weird enough, so that it does not limit God's freedom to make it what he pleases."[14] The body can be anything God wants it to be. Human beings can be embodied by God in myriad ways.

The second inference is this: The notion of the spiritual body of the resurrection—the spiritual body of Jesus as "the first fruits of those who have died" (1 Corinthians 15:20) and the spiritual bodies of the general resurrection—is possible even from the standpoint of philosophy. The image of the spiritual body of the resurrection is not more "strange" that some of the various depictions of body made by various theorists. The resurrection of Jesus cannot be proven as one would prove a theorem in geometry, but it can be shown to be compatible with human reason that is partnered with a paradigmatic religious imagination.

Finally, given the concepts of symbol and reality, and Bergson's concepts of the "body for itself" and "body for others," it is possible to imagine the risen Jesus as being really present in Church, Word, and Sacrament. The ideas of symbol and reality are often opposed as representing two distinct poles of a dichotomy. If something is a symbol, it is frequently thought to be a "mere" symbol or something that simply stands for some reality that is genuinely absent. If something is present in all of its actuality, it is thought to be factual and opposed to symbolic. The distinction between what is symbolic and actual, I submit, is a false distinction.

There is a justification etymologically to interpret the Greek *symbolon* as a token of identity and, by extension, an expression of presence. If, for example, in ancient Greece, a person produced half a coin, that individual's identity was established when the broken coin was matched by an arbiter against its other half. Now imagine that everyone's "body for others" (the physical body of definite form and dimension) is, after a manner of speaking, the other half of the person's "body for itself." To be more explicit, a person's "body for others" is the symbol of that person's "body for itself," the body that is coextensive with the individual's consciousness. The symbol that is my actual physical body is, of course, ineluctably joined to the reality of my body that "reaches to the stars" in

Bergson's phrase. What is viewed as my real body by others is real, but it is also (from another point of view) a token that stands for my "body for itself." My physical body of definite form and dimension is denotative of my body without definite form and dimension. I suggest that Bergson's distinction makes sense only when the "body for others" is recognized as the symbol of "the body for itself."

Concluding Remarks

The risen and glorified body of Jesus is present symbolically, but not less really, in Church, Word, and Sacrament. These are Jesus' "bodies for others" in today's world. (His "body for itself" reigns now with his Father in heaven). Jesus is really present in modes of presence that transcend human understanding and all available language. To demand a presence that fits *known* human categories before it can be termed real, a presence that can be expressed in finite language, is to exercise a childish whim instead of a developed spirituality and critical sense regarding a divine mystery. Christ is really present in symbolic—but no less real—form in Church, Word, and Sacrament. He is at work gracing the world with his blessings.

Notes to Appendix B

1. Caroline Walker Bynum, *The Resurrection of the Body in Western Christianity, 200-1336* (New York: Columbia University Press, 1995.
2. Benedict Ashley, *Theologies of the Body: Humanist and Christian* (Braintree, MA: Pope John Center, 1985-95).
3. Antoine Vergote, "The Body as Understood in Contemporary Thought and Biblical Categories," in *Philosophy Today*, 35, 1, 1991, 93-105.
4. Ibid., 94.
5. Ibid., 96.
6. F. J. Taylor, "Body," ed. Alan Richardson, *A Theological Word Book of the Bible* (New York: Macmillan, 1967), 34.
7. Antoine Vergote, "The Body as Understood in Contemporary Thought and Biblical Categories," 98.
8. Ibid., 99.
9. Ibid., 103.
10. Kenneth Grayson, "Body," ed. Alan Richardson, *A Theological Word Book of the Bible,* 83.

11. Antoine Vergote, "The Body as Understood in Contemporary Thought and Biblical Categories," 101.
12. John C. Mullarkey, "Duplicity in the Flesh: Bergson and the Current Philosophy of Body," in *Philosophy Today*, 38, 4, 1994, 339-355.
13. Henri Bergson, *Creative Evolution,* trans. Arthur Mitchell (New York: The Modern Library, 1944), 380-384.
14. Freeman Dyson, *Infinite in All Directions* (New York: Harper and Row, 1989), 8.

INDEX OF SUBJECTS

INDEX OF NAMES

34168072R00107

Made in the USA
Lexington, KY
25 July 2014